W9-BTS-617

Stan Smith's
Winning Doubles

Stan Smith's Winning Doubles

Stan Smith

Human Kinetics

Library of Congress Cataloging-in-Publication Data

Smith, Stan, 1946–
  [Winning doubles]
  Stan Smith's winning doubles / Stan Smith.
      p. cm.
Includes index.
  ISBN 0-7360-3007-7
  1. Tennis--Doubles. I. Title.
  GV1002.8 .S65 2002
  796.342'28--dc21   2002002156

ISBN-10: 0-7360-3007-7
ISBN-13: 978-0-7360-3007-6

Acquisitions Editor: Martin Barnard; **Developmental Editor:** Julie Rhoda; **Assistant Editor and Copyeditor:** Carla Zych; **Proofreader:** Sarah Wiseman; **Indexer:** Sharon Duffy; **Graphic Designer:** Fred Starbird; **Graphic Artist:** Kimberly McFarland; **Photo Manager:** Les Woodrum; **Cover Designer:** Jack W. Davis; **Photographer (cover):** Andrea Renault/Globe Photos, Inc.; **Photographers (interior):** Photos on pages 13, 31, 36, 45, 54-56, 67-72, 75, 78-79, 96-101, 103-105, 110, 115-117, and 125 © Fred Mullane/Cameraworks, Inc. All other photos by Tom Roberts.; **Art Manager**: Carl Johnson; **Illustrator:** Accurate Art; **Printer**: United Graphics

Printed in the United States of America   10   9   8   7   6   5

Human Kinetics
Web site: www.HumanKinetics.com

United States: Human Kinetics, P.O. Box 5076, Champaign, IL 61825-5076
800-747-4457
e-mail: humank@hkusa.com

Canada: Human Kinetics, 475 Devonshire Road, Unit 100, Windsor, ON N8Y 2L5
800-465-7301 (in Canada only)
e-mail: orders@hkcanada.com

Europe: Human Kinetics, 107 Bradford Road, Stanningley
Leeds LS28 6AT, United Kingdom
+44 (0) 113 255 5665
e-mail: hk@hkeurope.com

Australia: Human Kinetics, 57A Price Avenue, Lower Mitcham, South Australia 5062
08 8372 0999
e-mail: liaw@hkaustralia.com

New Zealand: Human Kinetics, Division of Sports Distributors NZ Ltd.
P.O. Box 300 226 Albany, North Shore City, Auckland
0064 9 448 1207
e-mail: info@humankinetics.co.nz

To all the coaches who have helped me in my career,
particularly Pancho Segura, George Toley, and Dennis Ralston;

to my two main doubles partners, Erik van Dillen and
the guy who has carried me for over 30 years, Bob Lutz;

and to my mom, my dad, and my two brothers, Ken and Steve,
without whose encouragement and support I would not have even
begun playing this great game

Contents

Introduction

Doubles has been a big part of my tennis career. It has provided me with the opportunity to play as part of a team, which is the way I first became involved in sports. I started playing basketball, football, and baseball as part of a team, and fellowship with my teammates is what made my early participation in sports fun.

I have learned a great deal about playing doubles through my junior, college, and professional playing and coaching experiences. I have been fortunate enough to play with some very good doubles players, including my most frequent doubles partner, Bob Lutz. I have played in 11 Grand Slam event finals, and all but 3 of them were with Bob. Bob and I also won the NCAAs twice as a doubles team many years ago. Needless to say, we have gotten to know each other's games unbelievably well, and this has helped us win some tight matches. Bob is a great doubles player because he serves consistently, he volleys well, he returns serve solidly, and he knows how to play the angles of the doubles court as well as any player in the game. We still play together in the senior Grand Slam events, and it continues to be fun for us to compete against some very familiar rivals.

Today most people who play tennis play doubles, probably because doubles is more physically forgiving as well as more social, and therefore more fun. My goal in writing this book is to give you some specific help with your doubles game based on my experiences and observations of many levels of play. I hope that this advice will not only make you a more effective and successful doubles player but will also increase your enjoyment of the game.

There is an old saying that the most important aspect of a doubles match is the choosing of a partner. It's a little like dating; you want to find the best possible partner, someone who can shore you up in crucial situations, while at same time your partner is trying to find someone as good as or better than he or she is to provide support when things get tough. Each player would like to have all the individual characteristics and skills of a good doubles player and would also like to have a partner with all the right stuff. In the less than ideal real world, a player may have specific shortcomings that call for a partner with offsetting attributes. I will help you work through this dating-game dilemma so that you can forge a successful marriage. I'll also provide some strategies to help you make your doubles team marriage work more effectively. I'll discuss how to improve communication with your partner on and off the court and ways to devise strategies for your game that will highlight your team's strengths while downplaying your weaknesses.

The best doubles players and the best doubles teams share several characteristics. They include the following:

- The ability to serve consistently and accurately
- The ability to quickly follow the serve to the net
- Solid volleying skills
- Quick hands
- The ability to anticipate your opponents' shots
- A knack for ideal positioning
- An aggressive on-court nature
- The ability to return serves dependably
- The ability to make adjustments
- A good sense of how to use the whole court
- An enjoyment of team play

Bob Lutz and I realized soon after we started playing together that his strengths supported my weaknesses and vice versa. I played more aggressively than he did, but I was not consistent. He was more dependable with his returns of serve, and I helped him at the net when he was serving. We both had pretty quick hands and were able to adjust our strategy during a match. We had several options at our disposal, and we used the style of play that we felt would be most effective for the particular situation. We were able to come to the net behind our return or to return and stay back. When playing the deuce side, I would sometimes run around my backhand on a second serve, hit a low forehand return, and continue going to the center of the court, and Bob would cross and intercept the first volley. If the point did not end with his volley, I would then cover the left side of the court, and he would cover the right. If we weren't returning well, we would both stay back on the first serve to try to make the other team hit a few more balls. If our opponents were not hitting the return down the line, one of us would play close to the center of the court while the other was serving in order to make the return area smaller and put more pressure on the returner. When we were not doing well, we would poach more to get ourselves more actively involved in the game so that we were dictating instead of being dictated to. We both enjoyed the thrill of team victory, and neither of us liked the agony of defeat.

Tennis has changed quite a bit over the years, in part because of changes and improvements in equipment. Players are able to hit the ball harder and more accurately than ever with today's bigger, stronger, lighter, and longer rackets. Doubles tennis today includes more aggressive returns of serve, less defensive lobbing, more offensive lobbing, more poaching, and bigger serving than in the past. I'll discuss ways that you can take advantage of the new equipment.

There are other ways you can get an edge on your competition as well. I'll talk about how you can make changes to your doubles game through stroke production, strategy, conditioning, nutrition, mental toughness, and other means that will help you improve. I'll offer tips and examples from my experience playing, coaching, and observing doubles tennis as well as some stories about what the pros have done to win more doubles matches.

I've played against or observed closely some of the great players of all time, players such as Billie Jean King, Margaret Court, Chris Evert, Martina Navratilova, Martina Hingis, Rod Laver, Bjorn Borg, Jimmy Connors, John McEnroe, and Pete Sampras. Throughout their careers these players continued to work on their games and make little changes so that they could be more competitive. Not one of these great players was ever satisfied with his or her game. Whether they played singles or doubles, these players knew that they had to continue to improve or they would be toppled.

Doubles presents communication issues that simply don't come up in singles. For example, doubles players can discuss tactics and strategy before, during, and after a match. They can encourage each other directly on the court, which may prevent them from freezing up, giving up, or just plain losing it during a difficult match.

Sometimes two good singles players will play doubles as if they were on a singles court. Not only will such a team not be as effective as it could be, but it may provide comic relief for the opponents and fans. It's always fun to see both members of a team let the ball go down the middle or, even better, to see both players go for the same ball. In one big Davis Cup match in Romania, our opponents got so mad at each other that after the first set they stopped talking to each other. Needless to say, their ordinarily high level of play suffered as a result of their complete lack of communication.

On the other hand, the great teams like Martina Navratilova and Pam Shriver, Peter Fleming and John McEnroe, John Newcombe and Tony Roche, Todd Woodbridge and Mark Woodforde, Gigi Fernandez and Natasha Zvereva have been described as peanut butter and jelly, or a horse and carriage. They offer each other encouragement, motivation, calm, excitement, distraction, a fitting joke, empathy, and friendship as needed. I will point out some of the specific ways that such professional doubles players work well together so that you can put their techniques to work for you.

Older players may find that they can play doubles more effectively than singles because they don't have to cover as much court, and they can use a variable strategy to make up for reduced power and mobility. For the 50 and over player, the game changes a little with the onset of a few aches and pains, but it can be as much or more fun than ever. As an active player in this category (is it possible that I am really eligible to play in this league?), I have found that if I stay in reasonably good shape, I can play at a relatively high level through smart positioning on the court and good shot selection. Most players this age have a wealth of experience, so hitting the right shots may just be a matter of having a good memory. Whether or not they have a good memory, older players can always improve and take advantage of their opponents' diminishing skills.

I hope that you enjoy not only reading this book but also putting these tips into practice so that you can enjoy this great game and be a more successful player.

Building a Winning Doubles Team

Doubles is the game most tennis players play today, but too many players play doubles as if they were playing singles on a doubles court. I have seen several really good singles players who just do not have a clue how to play a doubles match. Cliff Richey, a top player during my era, is a case in point. He was the number-one singles player in the United States, but when he got on the doubles court he would run right down the center of the court toward the net with no regard as to where his partner was positioned. Sometimes he would hit a winner, and sometimes he would hit his partner. In the latter case, he might or might not focus on his partner long enough to apologize before moving on to the next point. I kind of enjoyed watching his doubles matches because they featured some pretty good comedy, but each show usually lasted just one round, and then Cliff was back to playing singles.

When you evaluate the differences between singles and doubles, it is important to consider the essential elements of each game. These essentials include strategy, conditioning, mental toughness, quick hands and feet, and the skills required in serving, volleying, returning the serve, hitting ground strokes, lobbing, and moving around the net. Your personality will also help determine whether you will lean toward singles or doubles. Table 1.1 may help you decide if you have what it takes to play effective doubles.

Understanding Doubles Strategy

Knowing and understanding the differences between singles and doubles strategy and tactics is a key to becoming a better doubles player, whether you are playing doubles or mixed doubles. For example, some moves that work on the singles court but are not as effective in a doubles game are those big, freewheeling returns of serve, serving and then staying back, returning serve down the middle, and staying back on the baseline waiting for a mistake. If you use these moves, then you will be easy pickings for a good doubles team. Big, hard returns are more difficult to hit consistently in doubles tennis, and good volleyers can handle them pretty well. Good doubles players don't stay back after serves but instead approach the net. They also keep returns of serve away from the middle.

Playing singles tennis is a great challenge because there is no one to help you during a match. If you are losing, then you have to figure out how to change your tactics, strategy, or level of play, or you will surely come in second. Some players have the ability to do this, and others freeze up or have trouble figuring out how to adjust their play to fit their opponent or the conditions. Players who have difficulty adjusting their singles game during tough matches may do quite well in doubles play because they have another player to help them determine what to do. Such players may also feel less pressure on the court because they are not alone and may appreciate having a partner to encourage them when a match starts "going south."

Throughout this book I describe how to plan and analyze your doubles strategy, especially how to troubleshoot when a match is not going well. Communication, discussed in chapter 2, is one of the most important keys to playing successful doubles tennis as well as one of the biggest differences between singles and doubles. Adapting your positioning on the court as described in chapter 3 will allow you to optimize your team's strategy, make the most of your strengths, and protect your weaknesses. For example, if you have a big forehand and not much of a backhand, you should change your positioning when receiving second serves in order to attack with your strongest weapon and avoid hitting a lot of backhands. Serving strategies, covered in chapter 4, are a bit different in doubles play. There are returning strategies (see chapter 5) to counteract the particular challenges of doubles

Table 1.1

Elements of Success in Singles Versus Doubles Tennis

Elements of Success	Singles	Doubles
Strategy	Move opponents from corner to corner. Be steady.	Make opponents volley up. Gamble more with poaches.
Mental toughness	Can depend only on yourself during match	Partner can help support you
Conditioning		
Aerobic	Very important in long matches	Less necessary than in singles
Speed	Very important	Important, especially when moving at the net
Strength	Important, especially if you are a power player	Depends on style of play. If you are a finesse player, not as important as speed.
Quickness	Can get away with not coming to net as much	Need to be able to reflex balls back and recover quickly
Skills		
Serve	Go for first serve, but have a secure second serve	Take pace off first serve to get higher percentage in. Get to net fast behind serve.
Volley	Generally volley hard and hard and deep. Occasional drop volley.	Volley is important and will vary. Some hard and deep, more angles, and accurate shots at opponent's feet.
Return of serve	Hard and deep, or high and deep if opponent stays back. Short and at feet if opponent comes in.	Short and at opponent's feet, keep low. Hard and deep if server stays back.
Groundstroke	Heavy and deep	More variety and angles
Lob	Not used very much	Can be very useful
Poach	Not used at all	Very important
Drop shot	Can be effective	Not used very much
Drop volley	Helpful if you are a server and volleyer	Can be very helpful to be able to hit angle drop volley

tennis, such as staying back and making opponents who are known as big serving teams hit more volleys without a human target. In chapter 6 I explain the variety of volleys and angle shots that doubles players can take advantage of. The doubles team can be better than the sum of its parts (the talents of the individual singles players) if the members of the team have good doubles instincts and apply sound doubles strategy.

The high level of play exhibited by Lindsay Davenport is the result of solid conditioning as well as exceptional skills and talent. Here she gets low for a backhand groundstroke.

Conditioning for Doubles

An issue that comes into play whenever you are on court, whether you're playing singles or doubles, is conditioning. There are different types of conditioning that all work together to prepare you for your ideal performances. Some of these types include aerobic or endurance conditioning, which deals with your body's ability to take in oxygen as fast as your muscles need it and which generally translates into your stamina on the court; speed and quickness conditioning, which allows you to move where and when you need to on the court and to step and swing with appropriate timing; and strength conditioning, which ensures that you play with power and which helps you offset injuries. In chapter 7 I'll discuss specific ways to work these types of conditioning into a solid and complete practice, but the following paragraphs cover the basic essentials of all-around conditioning for doubles.

- **Aerobic conditioning.** Covering the whole court when playing singles requires the ability to not only move quickly, but to move quickly for a long distance during the course of a match. Singles players may run over five miles during a match. Most of that moving is made up of quick stop and start movements, which can take quite a bit out of you over the course of a match. With only 25 seconds between points in which to recover, the contest sometimes becomes more of a test of endurance than skill.

Now, in doubles, you don't have to move as far for each shot or as frequently over the course of a match, and therefore you will not tire as quickly as you would in a singles match. In doubles you will move only about two miles during a long match because the rallies are shorter, you are covering only half the court, and you are mainly going from baseline to net rather than across the baseline as you would in singles. The action of doubles can be fast and furious, requiring great reflexes, good positioning, proper shot selection, and keen anticipation. Certainly it helps to move well, but since you don't have to cover as much court as you would in singles, you can get away with not being in ideal aerobic condition. You should be able to last longer playing doubles than singles, and sometimes you may have to! I played one Davis Cup doubles match in which my partner and I were on the court for six hours on Saturday and still didn't finish the match. (We ended up playing the last set and a half on Sunday.) Believe me, even though it was *just* doubles, I was really tired by the end of that day.

- **Speed conditioning.** While aerobic conditioning is not needed as much for doubles play as it is for singles, speed conditioning is vital for both. The need to get to the net quickly and in good balance is the emphasis. After the serve you generally must sprint the first three steps, then split step to get your balance, then make a cut to hit the first volley. Speed work on or off the court, including ball drills, volleying, hitting overheads, and other exercises that I will describe in chapter 7, will help you prepare to execute these moves. Speed conditioning drills can help singles players, but they are particularly beneficial for doubles players because of the aggressive serve-and-volley aspect of the doubles game.

- **Strength conditioning.** All tennis players—singles and doubles players—need to have a good general strength program. It is particularly important for players to build and maintain strength in the legs, back, stomach, arms, and shoulders. As you can see, that just about covers every major muscle of the body.

As you begin your conditioning for the season, there are many things you can do that will help you compete at your best. Keep in mind that, as a doubles player, you are looking primarily to develop speed, quickness, and explosiveness. One of my favorite sports medicine doctors once stated that, "you should get in shape to play tennis, not play tennis to get in shape." This is cogent advice. I have known people who start playing hard before they are really ready because they want to shed some pounds or tone up quickly. When players go at it in this fashion they make themselves more vulnerable to injury, which can delay the start of the tennis season for them or even keep them out for the whole season. These people are usually type A personalities who are used to getting things done quickly. I cannot emphasize enough the importance of getting in shape gradually for the long, tough matches you will face.

So at the start of the season, about four to six weeks before your first match, do some long-distance running to gradually condition your cardiovascular system. For example, in college, during the first four weeks of our training, my coach, George Toley, would have us run a few miles every other day and then do a variety of calisthenics, some duckwalking and stretching, and a few sprints. As the weeks progressed, we would gradually do less long-distance running but more sprinting.

Running a combination of 400s, 600s, and 50-yard sprints along with strength training for the legs, back, shoulders, and arms will build a beginning fitness base. After about six weeks, you'll be ready to add on-court speed and quickness work in order to be ready for the season. You can improve your fitness level by doing several more sprints, jumping rope, and doing some ball drills a couple of times a week. When you feel better about your overall fitness level, you can move on to some speed and strength work. Once a solid base of fitness is in place, a doubles player needs to emphasize endurance less than a singles player would, but do a good amount of quickness, reflex, and serve-and-volley work. Chapter 7 details some specific workouts appropriate for the different phases of the seasons.

In addition to overall conditioning, players should also do a proper warm-up. The warm-up before practice or a match sets the tone for the whole day (I cover a specific warm-up routine in chapter 7). Each time you run or play tennis, make sure that you warm up and stretch all the major muscles so that you reduce your risk of injury. The worst thing that can happen to an excited tennis enthusiast is to have the time and interest to play but wind up sidelined, spending time in rehab nursing an injury that could have been prevented with just a few minutes of warming up and stretching.

Assessing Your Strengths and Weaknesses

As you start your search for a partner it is important to consider first how *you* play. You must be honest with yourself as far as your strengths and weaknesses are concerned. The better you know your own personality and style of play, the easier it will be to understand what you are looking for in a partner. I believe this is an interesting process that can be helpful to you in your tennis game as well as other areas of your life.

So how do you figure out your strengths and weaknesses? A good way to start is, of course, by analyzing your own game. Now, self-analysis may or may not be totally accurate. A player may claim to be a really good doubles player simply because his partnership had a good season. The reality is that the player's partner was so good that the team was successful *in spite* of his own weaknesses. Or someone may claim to serve and volley well because she always holds the serve when playing with a particular partner. The fact of the matter is that her partner is so effective at the net that he is winning most of the points for the team by poaching; without a clever partner, that server would be very average. Table 1.2 will help you perform an honest, accurate self-analysis by asking you to rate each element of your game.

When you analyze your game it is also important to think about your personality and the type of attitude you have on the court. For example, are you someone who likes to compete and who enjoys the pressure, or do you need help in this regard from a stronger personality or a player with a more positive attitude? Generally one player is a little more of a cheerleader than the other, and that seems to make a good blend for a team. Todd Woodbridge and Mark Woodforde, who won the Wimbledon doubles five times in a row, have different temperaments and, in different situations, each one played an important emotional role for the team. When they were a bit flat and sluggish, then Todd would get them pumped up. If things got too exciting and there were some conflicts taking place on the court, Mark would exert a calming influence. Are you the high-fiver or chest-bumper type, or are you a little more laid back? Knowing yourself can help you determine the type of personality you want playing beside you, the type of player who will complement your strengths and weaknesses.

It is sometimes helpful to get other opinions of your game and personality to give you a better idea of just where you stand as far as your true strengths and weaknesses. I would suggest that you get together with your club's pro

Table 1.2

Doubles Self-Assessment Questionnaire

Rate each element on a scale of 1-5.

5	Excellent	> 80%
4	Good	71% to 80%
3	Average	56% to 70%
2	Poor	40% to 55%
1	Unacceptable	< 40%

Skill	Question	Essential Element to Rate	Score (1-5)
Serve	How effective is my first serve?	Speed and power	
		Percentage in	
		Accuracy of placement	
		Ability to vary the spin	
		Ability to serve from different positions on baseline	
	How effective is my second serve?	Speed and power	
		Dependability—should be able to keep opponents at least in a neutral mode	
		Accuracy of placement	
Following serve to the net	How quickly can I get to the net?	Percentage you **don't** have to half volley	
	Can I cover most returns with good balance?	Percentage covered	
	Is my first volley dependable?	Percentage of first volleys hit in	
	Do I need help at the net?	Percentage of first volleys hit in	
Return of serve—first shot	Can I return cross-court consistently?	Percentage of cross-court returns	
	Can I hit a variety of types of returns (rate each)?	Block	
		Drive	
		Chip and charge	
		Down the line	
		Lob	
	Can I hit a return at opponent's feet?	Percentage of returns at feet	

Skill	Question	Essential Element to Rate	Score (1-5)
Return of serve— second shot	Can I hit a variety of shots (rate each)?	Drive down the middle Short angle Down the line Offensive lob	
	How are my defensive skills when forced out of position?	Rate defensive skills	
Server's partner	How helpful am I to my partner when I am at the net?	Rate helpfulness	
	Am I quick enough?	Rate quickness	
	Am I aggressive enough?	Rate aggressiveness	
	Can I cover my own lobs?	Percentage of lobs covered	
	Can I poach well off a good return?	Percentage of successful poaches	
Mental preparation	Do I need support during a match?	Rate emotional control	
	Do I think well under pressure?	Rate troubleshooting ability	
Physical condition	Do I get tired early in a match?	Rate aerobic fitness	
	Do I need more strength?	Rate strength	
	Do I need more quickness?	Rate speed and quickness	

and ask his or her opinion of where you are strong in your doubles game and where you could use some work. The pro could also give you a suggestion as to what type of player might be good for you at this point in your career. If you don't work with a pro, then you may want to ask a player who is a few levels higher than you to assess the good and bad points of your game. If you don't know anyone like that, then talk to some of your buddies with whom you play and get their opinions about the specific areas outlined in the checklist (table 1.2). If you have a group with whom you play regularly, then there probably aren't any secrets that they would hesitate to share.

Finding a Partner

Once you figure out your strengths and weaknesses, it is important to find a player who can complement your style of play, personality, technique, and athletic ability. The first and foremost reason to pick a partner is that he or she is someone with whom you are going to enjoy your time on the court. I hate to bring up an old cliché, but it *is* only a game. In Webster's (Merriam-Webster's Collegiate Dictionary, 10th Edition), the first definition of *game* is "diversion or amusement," followed by "fun, sport." It doesn't make sense to play with someone with whom the time spent is barely tolerable. You can go to the dentist for that. Remember that doubles can be more fun than singles precisely because it is truly a team sport. The variety of personalities and shots in doubles should increase your enjoyment of the game. There are enough things that you have to do in life that are not enjoyable; why would you deliberately put yourself in a situation with someone who rubs you the wrong way? Now that the true reason to play the game is clear in your mind, let's look at some other issues to ponder as you look for that ideal courtmate.

Style of Play

If you are not very quick but have a good solid game, then you should look for a partner who can move well and take advantage of your good returns and consistency. This player may not be as solid in performing skills or as consistent in making shots but may like to take chances by moving to take advantage of a set of opportunities to finish the point decisively. The player who takes the chances may miss occasionally, but his or her movement and daring will make the other team apprehensive every time they have to stretch for a difficult shot. This type of play often pays off in critical situations such as break points. The other team might try to go behind the crossing player, assuming that he or she is on the move, and either try to hit too good a shot or hit right into the waiting racket of their opponent. It is beautiful to watch an experienced team play like this and set up the big point for the kill.

If your style of play is erratic and you like to take chances, then look for a partner who is more consistent and conservative to balance your style. This combination always causes problems for the opposition and thus can be very effective. I played with Bob Lutz for most of my career. Bob was the steady player, and I was the one who liked to take the chances. He would rarely miss a return of serve when he was playing well, and I would move around the net trying to intimidate our opponents and take advantage of his great shots. When he served, I was always looking to cross and keep the other team guessing. Sometimes I would get burned by crossing, and the other guys would hit a winner behind me. But when it came to a big point, they didn't know if I was going to poach or not. Sometimes they would try

John McEnroe–Peter Fleming

John McEnroe and Peter Fleming dominated the men's doubles scene during the late 1970s because they effectively combined two elements—power and finesse. The joke in those days was that McEnroe and anybody was the best team in the world, as McEnroe was actually a better doubles player than he was a singles player (and he was a great singles player). But the joke does not give proper credit to Fleming. Together they won many titles against good teams, and Peter's play was usually the determining factor in the outcome. If he played well, then they were really tough, almost unbeatable. If he did not play well, then the other guys had a slight chance.

As on most lefty-righty teams, the left-hander, "Mac," played the ad side of the court while the right-hander, "Big Flem," played the deuce. I have never seen a great team with a right-hander and a left-hander who played the other way around.

Their style of play was aggressive, especially from the Fleming point of view. Peter, at 6' 5", would rocket the serve. His problem was that he would sometimes lose his rhythm and serve a few double faults. He had a "take no prisoners" mentality that would carry over from the serve to the other parts of his game. On the return, he had a nice, aggressive, driving backhand; when it was good, it was very good. He would slash at the forehand, which made that side spotty but dangerous. McEnroe had a very difficult serve to read, and the left-handed slice kept opponents off balance all the time. He could hit with power, but he also had soft hands that gave him terrific control of the ball. John would go through periods in which he just would not make an unforced error. If he did make one, you would not have to guess what had happened; his reaction to such an occurrence was always conspicuous and easy to interpret.

McEnroe–Fleming was by far the fieriest of the great doubles teams. Sometimes they would really lose their cool, and anything might happen. Peter was hard on himself. The only person harder on himself was John. Together, Peter and John won many titles. They were most effective on the faster surfaces, but they could play on anything. They supported each other and knew how to take advantage of each other's great shots. Often Peter or John would poach and put tremendous pressure on the first volley after the serve. With Peter's long wingspan, he could reach more balls than anyone else in the game.

to hit too good a return and would miss. Sometimes they would hit the ball right to me, and I would put away the volley. Many times they would take their eyes off the ball, looking to see what I was going to do, and mis-hit it feebly into the net. Of course, they would make a great shot occasionally, and that was the chance we took. But by intimidating our opponents and keeping them unsure of what we were going to do, uncertain as to whether and when I would move, we kept them off balance and won some easy points.

Some players like to play close to the net so that they can knock off any volley on which they can get their racket. This is not the ideal way to play, but if you choose to do so, then you need to find someone who is capable of covering the lobs that get over your head. If you like to camp on the net, then I suggest that you learn a very important word, which if overused may not make you the most popular doubles partner in your group. That word, of course, is "yours."

Players who don't do well covering their own overheads generally don't practice moving backward very much. I once did a clinic in Atlanta for a group of women who were relatively new players. Their pro had taught them to volley first and then to hit groundstrokes. I would serve and come to the net to play out the doubles points, and every one of the women would hit the return of serve and come to the net behind it. I could not believe my eyes! Then I found out that they would practice hitting overheads and volleys during every lesson they took. These women covered most of their own overheads when they played matches. You don't have to be quick or tall to be able to do that. You just have to anticipate and practice going back for the overhead and returning to the net for the next shot.

Personality

If you have a tendency to get down on yourself on the court, then you should find a partner who can be very positive and supportive when things get tough. That person may be more talkative than you and keep you more relaxed in those high-pressure situations that you run into during close matches. I have seen players get so despondent that it takes a partner with the ability to break through the mood to get that player back on track. Unfortunately, some players get into a funk and stay in it for the rest of the match no matter what their partners say or do. If you find yourself feeling this way, try to sit down and address the situation with your partner and see if you can talk it through. Now this can happen to anyone once in a while, and you shouldn't panic when it does if your partnership has generally been enjoyable and successful. If it happens too many times, though, you should look for a partner with a more consistently positive attitude.

Perhaps you don't get despondent or discouraged, but you do get extremely tense in crucial situations. Now, the first thing to know is that *every* player gets nervous at some point or another; it happens to the best players in the world at various times in their career. When Rod Laver was serving for the match at Forest Hills (the US Nationals) to win the Grand Slam for the *second* time, he said that he could barely get his racket back on his serve.

When John McEnroe was at match point against Ivan Lendl to win the French Championships, he missed an easy volley that he will never forget. Chrissie Evert used to say that if her hands didn't get sweaty before a big match, then she probably wouldn't play as well. The point here is that it is *normal* to get nervous or tense when you get into critical situations. The key is to understand what happens to you and to figure out how to handle those situations better.

Encouraging words from a supportive partner can inspire confidence and calm nerves. A supportive gesture, such as the congratulatory high-five I'm shown here giving to my son, Ramsey, can have the same effect.

Some players get so nervous, though, that they can hardly move their legs, and their mobility suffers. Others can barely move their arms, and they lose power and spin. Most people tend to rush and make careless errors trying to get the point over with quickly. A few people overhit and spray their shots all over the fences. In tense situations try instead to take your time, make sure that you continue to breathe, determine an appropriate game plan so that there is limited doubt in your mind as you hit the ball, and give yourself some positive self-talk. As far as the type of partner you should pick if you tend to get very nervous, look for someone who is confident and encouraging on the court. Just playing doubles rather than singles should take some of the pressure off, and having a partner who will be positive and talk you through tight situations will really lighten your load.

Mixed Doubles

What can I say about mixed doubles, except don't play such a game? Just kidding! This game does present some unique challenges that do not exist in men's doubles and women's doubles. I'll talk specifically about some of these things in the chapter on communication. Many people do play with their spouses and have great relationships both on the court and off. I played with my wife Margie in the US National Championships twice before we were married. We didn't have great success, but we had fun. I think it was my fault that we didn't win; I didn't play very well. Unfortunately we have not competed as partners since we were married, but we have spent over 25 happy years together.

Picking Your Side

A key issue to think about as you construct your doubles team is which side of the court you prefer playing, the deuce or the ad side.

If you like to play the deuce court, you should look for a great left-hander as a partner. Many of the best partnerships over the years have been right-hander and left-hander combinations. Just a few examples of these teams are Newcombe and Roche, McEnroe and Fleming, Woodbridge and Woodforde, and Navratilova and Shriver. Almost always the left-hander plays the ad side in order to hit the second serve return and the second shot after the return of serve more readily with the forehand.

A common approach to determining sides on a doubles team is to have the stronger player play the ad, or backhand, side. This is because the game point is most likely to occur on that side, and you want your best chance to win that point. The problem with this plan is that you may not get to game point if you don't win points from the deuce side. The reason behind having the stronger player play the ad side is not bad, but there are some other factors to consider (see table 1.3).

When you are deciding whether to play together, it is important to understand that each of you may feel more comfortable playing one side of the court than the other. Some players feel that they can *only* play one side and would not even consider playing the other side. If this is the case, then obviously such a player is limited in selecting a partner. Now most players have a favorite side but are also able to play on the other side, giving the team some options as to how they might work together most effectively.

The reasons players prefer a particular side usually revolve around what their favorite shots are. For example, Bob Hewitt and Frew McMillan, one of the best teams of their time, always played the same side of the court. Bob played the deuce side, or first court, and Frew played the ad side, or second court. Bob had a very good inside-out backhand (the backhand hit from the deuce court that would be hit cross court) return of serve, which he would almost never miss. Now this is one of the hardest returns to hit, so a player who hits this shot well is valuable to a team and should play the deuce side. Frew was two-handed on both sides and was very effective in taking the hard serve early and hitting it down at the incoming server's feet. He would often follow the shot in and volley the next shot. I can't tell you how many times I was hit by one of Frew's two-handed volleys because it was so difficult to read where he was hitting the ball. With two hands on the racket, he could change the direction of the ball at the last minute. The key to playing against him was to keep him stretching so that he couldn't always get both hands on the racket. Because of their particular strengths, Bob and Frew were most effective playing their preferred sides all the time.

Some players have such great forehands that you would think they should always play on the deuce side, but this isn't necessarily the case. I have seen teams be very effective by having the player with the better forehand play the ad side and, on the second shot or return of serve, run around the backhand and hit a big, topspin forehand. Bob Lutz and I lost to such a team in the 1980 finals at Wimbledon, Australians Paul McNamee and Peter McNamara. Paul was very quick and would run around the second serve almost every time so that he could dip that ball at our feet with the forehand. If we did get the serve effectively to his backhand, he would try to hit it low so that we had to volley up to him, enabling him to hit the forehand on the second shot. If we got too close to the net after the first volley, he had a very good forehand topspin lob that he could zip over our heads.

If your team is a lefty-righty combination, as many of the great teams over the years have been, then you have a big advantage. First of all, the other team always has to adjust to receiving a different type of serve each service

Table 1.3

Checklist for Deciding Which Side to Play

If you are right-handed and you ...	then you may be best suited to play the ...
like to hit the forehand return cross court especially when attacking a second serve	deuce side
like to hit the off-forehand especially when attacking the second serve	ad side
can hit the off-backhand	deuce side
can come into the net behind the return better from one side with a chip return or aggressive return	ad or deuce side, depending on how well you hit each shot
want the "big point" or game point	ad side
from an offensive position, hit the second shot (after the return of serve) cross court better from your right forehand side	deuce side
from an offensive position, hit the second shot (after the return of serve) better from your left side	ad side
from a defensive position, hit the second shot (after the return of serve) better from your right side	deuce side
from a defensive position, hit the second shot (after the return of serve) better from your left side	ad side
poach better from your left side	deuce side
poach better from your right side	ad side

game. One time the serve curves in from the right, and another time it slides in from the left. Next, both players on a lefty-righty team have the opportunity to have the forehands on the outside so that any ball that is not hit down the middle by the other team can be hit with a forehand. This applies to the return of serve as well as the rest of the balls that are hit during a rally. Because most players are more lethal with the forehand, being able to hit more forehands can be a huge advantage. You have only to look at a few of the great teams to see that the lefty-righty combos were some of the best that ever stepped onto a court. Look at the Grand Slam titles of these three teams: Newcombe–Roche with four Wimbledon titles as well as one French and two Australian titles, McEnroe–Fleming with four Wimbledon titles and

If you are left-handed and you ...	then you may be best suited to play the ...
like to hit the forehand return cross court especially when attacking a second serve	ad side
like to hit the off-forehand especially when attacking the second serve	deuce side
can come into the net behind the return better from the right side with a chip return or aggressive return	ad or deuce side, depending on how well you hit each shot
can come into the net behind the return better from the left side with a chip return or aggressive return	ad or deuce side, depending on how well you hit each shot
want the "big point" or game point	ad side
from an offensive position, hit the second shot (after the return of serve) better from your right side	deuce side
from an offensive position, hit the second shot (after the return of serve) better from your left forehand side	ad side
from a defensive position, hit the second shot (after the return of serve) better from your right side	deuce side
from a defensive position, hit the second shot (after the return of serve) better from your left side	ad side
poach better from your left side	deuce side
poach better from your right side	ad side

three US Open titles, and Woodforde–Woodbridge with six Wimbledon titles (five consecutive). Another American team, an identical-twin combo, Bob and Mike Bryan, played from age 5 one way. A year after they turned pro they changed sides, and they have been much more successful playing that way (left-handed on the ad side). Changing sides offers the advantage of a fresh approach; players benefit from having a new challenge and from getting out of their rut.

I have played the deuce, or forehand, side for most of my career. Bob Lutz and Erik van Dillen, with whom I have played most of my career, have almost always played the ad, or backhand, side. I used to kid Bob that the backhand side was easier to play because it is more natural to hit the backhand return of serve cross court than to hit the off-backhand.

Parent–Child Play

Most children start playing tennis because of their parents' interest in the game. In many cases, parents will take children out to the court for their very first experience, even if it's just to watch their parents play. Ivan Lendl's parents brought him to the court when he was very young and put him on a leash that was hooked to the net post while they played. He says he soon wanted to get unattached and try playing tennis himself. I would not recommend that you use this particular method of introduction with your own offspring, but I do think that actually playing tennis with your children is a great way to show them how exciting and enjoyable the sport can be.

As children get older and develop greater interest in the game, the family can play together in a variety of combinations, such as brother–sister, mother–daughter, father–son, and so forth.

When you start playing with your child, you will naturally be the better player and will therefore have to lead the team. This can be a little tricky, because your child may not enjoy having you tell him or her what to do all the time. It is important to do a little less talking than you would in other parent–child situations and to focus on being as supportive as you would be if you were playing with an adult partner. This approach is more fun for both of you, and treating each other as partners encourages you and your child to play your best.

As your child gets older, you may find that the roles are reversed. The child may become the better player. I find this development to be really fun. When a youngster is truly an equal on the court, both the parent and child can learn from one another and enjoy the battle. I have had the opportunity to play some exhibition matches with my sons and daughters, and doing so has resulted in some wonderful experiences. The kids try hard and make some mistakes, just like adult partners, so I keep pretty quiet and play my own game. I occasionally give some advice, but not much more than I would offer another partner. Now my oldest two boys can hold their own when we play together. In fact, they are now stronger than I am (don't tell them I said that, though; I haven't yet admitted this to them), and I have to work hard to keep up my side of the deal.

I encourage you to play tennis with your children and, if possible, to get into some competitions together. This activity will keep you young, strengthen your relationship with your kids, and give you something to talk about for years to come.

But Bob could also play the deuce side. He enjoyed hitting the off-backhand from the deuce side, and naturally he had a better cross-court forehand because of his continental grip. Also, the second shot was better for his forehand because he had more options: the short cross-court angle, the hard drive down the middle, or a little late hit down the line. Bob also had more opportunities to hit the topspin lob on the second shot after the return of serve. When I played the ad side, I hit the backhand drive return better, and I could chip the return and come to the net more easily. After a little practice I could hit the off-forehand pretty well when I had time. I wasn't as good at hitting the second shot from that side.

Now, once you decide which side you want to play, realize that it is not an irrevocable decision. You may go through a period with your regular partner when you are struggling and are just not able to win the close matches. You may get a little bored with the side that you're playing and find that your partnership needs a change. Lutz and I went through this stage in 1979. We had won the US Open the year before but were not playing well leading up to that year's competition so we decided to switch sides. We played well on our new sides, enjoyed the change, and got to the finals, where we lost a close match to McEnroe and Fleming. The next year we went back to our normal formation and got some revenge against that same team in the finals. The moral of the story is not to be afraid to change sides and try playing the other way.

I guess the ultimate test of which player is the best partner for you is experience. I have seen some odd couples out there that no one would ever have guessed would be right for each other who have worked well together, have seemed to enjoy each other's company on the court, and have been very successful.

Considering the Surface of Play

One of the interesting things about tennis is that there are many different types of surfaces that dramatically alter the game. The basic surfaces are hard courts, clay, grass, and indoor carpets. Even surfaces within the same category can vary slightly, depending on the top surface. For example, hard courts can range from very fast-playing, slick cement to very slow-playing mixtures of top surface over asphalt. Clay courts in Europe are usually slower and lower bouncing than clay courts in the United States. The playing qualities of indoor courts typically depend on the carpet that is laid on the existing surface; if an indoor court has a permanent hard or clay surface it will play more like an outdoor court. Grass varies the least, of course, but plays differently if it is rolled very hard than if it is soft.

Generally, the playing surface affects doubles less than singles because the style of singles play itself varies much more than in doubles. In doubles, good teams try to serve and volley every time after the first serve and second serve, whereas in singles a player stays back more after a serve on a clay court or a slow, hard court than on a fast, hard court or grass court. Having said that, when playing on clay the return of serve team will be able to return better on a slow surface because they will have a split second more time to react. This puts a premium on serving better and volleying more accurately. Also, since clay has a loose top surface, movement is more difficult, especially for players who are not used to it or for players who hit too many shots when they are off balance.

Good players take advantage of slower surfaces by staying back on the return of serve and by making their opponents hit more volleys and more overheads. They will hit lobs off the return of serve and use the lob whenever they are in trouble during a rally. The reason for this strategy is that it is harder for opponents to put the overhead away on a slower court such as a clay court.

On the other hand, you will not see players who are playing on grass stay in the back court too long because they never know when they will get a bad bounce on the court. The servers try to serve and volley every serve, and those returning serve will try to take the net as soon as possible during the rally.

Communicating With Your Partner

The great advantage of doubles play over singles is that in doubles you are working together with your partner. You are not out there on your own trying to fight the battle and figure out what to do if things go south. The ideal situation is one in which you and your partner play as one and each of you knows exactly what the other is thinking all the time. In this ideal mode you can anticipate each shot and react in such a way as to take advantage of every shot.

Unfortunately, the ideal is just that. In the real world it takes a lot of communication to really know what your partner is likely to do in each and every situation on the court. Even if you do understand each other very well, you don't always hit the shot that you should or play as well as you would like. In this chapter I cover how you can enhance team communication before, during, and after matches to improve your doubles game. There is a great deal that you can do to enable your team to play better and to enjoy the experience even more than you do now.

Before the Match

Effective communication does not start as a match starts but before the match, in practice sessions, and off the court; this head start will make your on-the-court communication clearer and more effective. *How* you communicate is one thing, and *what* you discuss is another. You will want to talk through specific strategies you might want to use against your opponents and discuss how you feel about situations that could come up during a particular match.

When playing against most teams, you should prepare a couple different plans to switch to if your original game plan is not working as well as you would like. Be open with your partner and work together to analyze whether or not to implement a change. One of you may say, "OK, I am not returning serve as well as I had hoped, so let's both stay back when I am returning the first serve and see if we can get into more points." You may communicate strategy changes or suggestions in technique such as, "Try getting your racket back quicker on the return of serve," or you may communicate how you are feeling. You may be feeling quick and want to poach more, or you may not feel confident about serving and volleying on your second serve and prefer to stay back on the second serve. Communicate how you think the opponents are playing and what your team can do to take advantage of their type of play. You may just want to encourage your partner or to help him or her relax. A simple comment such as, "Isn't this fun?" or "This is what it is all about, let's go for it!" may help your team through a tight situation.

Evaluate Your Team's Strengths and Weaknesses

When two players get together, their individual strengths and weaknesses may combine to make a solid team. On the other hand, they may have many of the same weaknesses and therefore be very vulnerable in those areas as a team. An ideal situation occurs when one player is consistent, but slower, while the other is wilder in hitting shots, but quick; then the quicker one can poach a lot and take advantage of his partner's good shots. Talk with your partner about how each of you can contribute to the team.

Once you have decided to play together, spend some time discussing how you can be the best team possible. Talk about the individual strengths and weaknesses you assessed in chapter 1 and how they can mesh to your collective advantage. Analyzing the specific areas of the game one by one will give you a good idea of where you stand and where you can improve.

Table 2.1

Analyzing the Game

Area of the game	What to look for
Serving—first serve	Speed Spin Placement Percentage in
Serving—second serve	Offensive delivery Tendency to double-fault Ability to control placement Use of spin
Volleying	Ability to get in fast Ability to control volley Quick volley exchanges Quality of movement at the net as a team Ability to get back well for overheads
Return of serve	Ability to get returns in play Ability to attack second serves Ability to take advantage of partner's good return by poaching Ability to come to the net after the return
Support	Help and encouragement of partner Positive attitude Calm demeanor Ability to think about changes Enjoyment of battle
Defense	Ability to lob Ability to take pace off the ball Ability to reflex hard shots Ability to run the ball down

There are a couple different ways to go about reviewing this information. One way to clarify your thoughts is for you and your partner to write down your opinions on the strengths and weaknesses of both of your games. You can use the checklist provided in table 2.1 as a guide. Following this process will force both of you to think things through in a careful and organized manner. If your partner and you don't agree on what your respective strengths and weaknesses are, then you should both go through the process again. Your thoughts about how you play may not be entirely accurate or in line with those of your partner. Objectively discussing your respective attributes is always enlightening and generally very helpful. It is important to be honest with each other as well as open to your partner's input so that both of you can benefit from the feedback you get.

During this discussion, it is critical not to take each other's comments about your games personally. These comments have nothing to do with whether you are a good person or a bad person. They relate only to how you play the game. If you are overly sensitive to these opinions, it indicates that your self-worth is tied a little too closely to the level of your game. That is a problem you must resolve if you wish to improve your tennis skills, your doubles game, and your self-worth. Once you and your partner get over any differences of opinion, you are on your way to forming a productive relationship and to reaching your potential as a team.

Another way to reach a consensus of your individual strengths and weaknesses is to just talk through them without writing them down. Some people feel more comfortable doing this because it is easier for them to try to explain their thoughts conversationally than to try to put pen to paper. The important thing is that you are really clear with each other so that there are no misunderstandings or unvoiced expectations. As in other areas of life, the closer the expectations are to reality, the more comfortable everyone will feel in the long run. No matter how much discussion you have before you commence your partnership, there will be areas of understanding that need to be revised and improved as you compete side by side.

Each player may have opinions about how well the team is communicating and functioning, and a coach may have a different opinion based on what he or she is seeing and hearing during a match. A good coach can help a team understand what is generally expected, but the players' personalities will determine the ideal amount and type of communication that is best for their team. If you are not enjoying playing with a certain player, it may be that one of you has expectations that are not being met. The best way to evaluate the effectiveness of your team's communication is to sit down with your partner and a coach and spell out what your expectations are. Based on this information, the coach can offer some direction and can work with the players to discover whether there are irreconcilable differences or merely issues that can be resolved with some modification of behavior.

Having this discussion with your partner isn't just a one-time exercise. Good teams continue to evaluate their games periodically. I suggest that you take advantage of a logical break in your season or tournament schedule to use the checklist and reevaluate how things are going. If you are in a league competition, there are halfway points and breaks between seasons; these are logical times to reevaluate your team play.

Set Goals

You and your partner can set goals together to help motivate both of you to improve your areas of weakness and even your strengths. These goals should be specific, measurable, and realistic. Here is a list of possible goals:

- To win a higher percentage of first serve points when serving or when returning serve
- To win a higher percentage of second serve points when serving or when returning serve
- To keep a higher percentage of return of serves in play
- To get to the net faster and thus increase your percentage of volleys to half-volleys
- To hit a greater variety of serves (pace, spin, placement, and starting position)
- To win more points at the net
- To poach more often
- To try different on-court formations
- To encourage each other more

Bob Lutz and I played better when we moved at the net and communicated our intentions. Our Davis Cup captain would challenge us to talk to each other before each point. We got better at doing that, and our overall results improved.

It is good to write down your goals for several reasons. First, you will not forget them if they are listed on paper and you can refer to them easily. The very act of writing them down helps to ensure that you will both hold one another accountable. Whenever you feel a little discouraged, looking at and remembering your joint commitment to those goals will motivate you to keep pushing hard to attain them.

Once you have set your goals you can devise exercises that you can do individually or as a team to help you reach those goals. For example, if you feel that you need to make your forehand return of serve off the second serve more of a weapon, have your partner hit second serves to you and then you can move around and hit more forehand returns at him as he comes to the net. He can work on his serve and first volley while you work on hitting hard-driving forehand returns. Refer often to your specific and measurable goals so that you can monitor your progress. Practice drills are helpful, but ultimately, progress is measured by how well you perform during the heat of battle; no matter how much you pretend that you are playing in a big match, practice is not the same as the real thing.

Develop a Team Philosophy or Style

Each good tandem develops a team personality that reflects the team philosophy they believe in. By thinking about the way you want to approach the game of doubles—your team philosophy—you can identify the style of play that is best for your team. Your style should be based on playing high-percentage tennis and making the most of your team's strengths and weaknesses. High-percentage tennis involves selecting the shot in each situation that has the greatest likelihood of success. Playing the percentages doesn't mean that you will always win the point, however. Often the shot indicated by this style is not the most exciting or challenging shot possible, but it is the shot that will neutralize the point or set you up to win the point *most of the time.*

Bob Lutz and I decided early on that we were going to be aggressive players and that we'd try to take the net away from our opponents whenever we could. We poached quite a bit and tried to intimidate our opponents into making mistakes. I frequently moved around at net to take advantage of Bob's outstanding returns of serve. In general, I was more of a gambler,

The aggressive style of play favored by Venus Williams, pictured here, and her sister, Serena, capitalizes on their tremendous strength and energy.

Venus Williams–Serena Williams

Venus and Serena Williams are sisters who have had a huge impact on the tennis scene, playing both singles and doubles. They started out in Compton, California as talented little girls with big ambitions in tennis as well as other aspects of life. They did not travel the standard route of playing junior tennis tournaments in Southern California and then moving on to women's contests. Thus, they were criticized for not developing in the traditional and, some would say, proper way. They stirred up quite a bit of hype before they had any wins, and this premature publicity did not make them very popular with the other girls their age. Eventually, they grew into big, strong young women who play a very aggressive style of tennis.

Both are right-handed and use two hands to hit the ball on the backhand side. They are extremely athletic, they have very good serves, and they hit volleys well. The sisters serve and volley in singles periodically, and therefore they are more experienced at serve-and-volleying than most other women in doubles tennis today. When they play doubles, which they usually do only in Grand Slam events, they like to overpower their opponents with big serves, strong returns of serve, and a lot of poaching at the net. When they are both healthy and eager to play, they dominate the events in which they participate.

Ordinarily, Venus plays the backhand side, and Serena plays the deuce. Venus once said that, when playing mixed doubles, she would rather receive the serve on the big ad-in or ad-out points and would therefore prefer that her male partner play the deuce side. This is like Michael Jordan saying that he'd like to have the ball in crucial situations and especially for the last shot of the game. Serena is no wallflower either; she also loves competition. Both women enjoy the battle and are very confident that they can get the job done. These are two of the characteristics that make them such a good team.

Whether or not they will ultimately be considered one of the great teams of all time may depend on how many Grand Slam events they play together over the next few years. If they play enough of them, they will improve their ability to volley and will become better versed in the proper tactics of the doubles game. The Williams sisters, with their energy, power, and confidence, are fun to watch as they dominate in matches against good teams.

making a few mistakes along with my winners, while Bob was steadier and more consistent. Our roles would sometimes shift a little, depending on how each of us was playing. Sometimes I was the steady player and Bob would hit more winners. So our basic philosophy was to "take it to" our opponents, to be aggressive and to overpower them with strong serving and consistent returning of serves. If we got a second serve, then we would try to be aggressive in that department as well and go for big shots.

Other teams place more of an emphasis on finesse. The great Rafael Osuna and Tony Palafox, from Mexico, were such a team. They were quick around the net and could dink, lob, and angle better than anybody in the game. If you played against this team, you had to hit a really good shot or the ball would come back again and again—usually at your feet, over your head, or out to the side. They never hurt you with power, but they sliced and diced you, bringing you to a slow death. They wore big smiles after the match, win or lose, and they usually tried to console their opponents after their victory. When we played them, we couldn't believe that we could lose to a team that almost never hit the ball hard. On the bright side, we got a few free lessons from them early in our careers on how to integrate a little finesse into our own games.

Another style of play, an option that works well for two players who are not very comfortable at net, is to have both players stay back on the return of serve and make their opponents hit a lot of balls. This can be an effective approach if the team's groundstrokes are strong enough and if the opponents are not very proficient volleyers. This style is not strongly recommended for most doubles play, but if it is done well it can be effective. Players with big topspin shots who can dip the ball low and force their opponents to hit many difficult volleys can win, especially if they keep their opponents off balance by way of timely offensive and defensive lobs. The problem is that if the opponents can volley those shots consistently, then the team using this style of play usually comes up with the short end of the score. If this is your current style and you have had success playing this way, try to gradually integrate the net game into your partnership.

Bob Lutz and I played Guillermo Vilas and Jose-Luis Clerc in an indoor Davis Cup match in Memphis, Tennessee, in the late 1970s. These guys had great topspin groundstrokes that were very consistent and powerful. They would stay back against us and return at our feet to force us to hit up on the volley, then, when they got the high ball that they liked, they would try to blow one right through us or around us. For five sets we lunged and reflexed volleys back as best we could. In the end, after being down some match points, we managed to come out on top. The fact that we were playing on a fast indoor court made it more difficult for them to be as effective with this tactic as they would have been on a slower clay court.

Most teams develop a philosophy that is best for their specific team and then adjust that philosophy based on their opponents and the type of surface on which the match is played. So consider and discuss how you might make any necessary adjustments against your favorite opponents. The more well rounded you are as a team, the more options you can develop and use when your preferred strategy is not working.

Have a Captain

Most teams have a captain who takes charge when the going gets tough. The election of a captain does not have to be a formal decision but can evolve naturally over time. A team may have one leader for tactical decisions and another for emotional situations. Talk through your team strategy before the match, but be prepared to make some changes to it as the match progresses. Usually one player takes charge of when to make changes and how to integrate them into the flow of the match. This may not always be the same team member; it can vary with the situation. Each player's personality will affect his or her aptitude for captaincy.

Bob and I shifted the captaincy of our team when we played together. When he became discouraged, I would try to pick him up emotionally. He would often take on the other team when I was struggling with my return of serve or volleying. When he played too conservatively and failed to come to the net behind his return of serve, I would nudge him a bit. When I started returning badly, Bob would suggest that we both stay back on the first serve. Even today when we play, he can get pretty vocal if I lob volley a few too many times or if my lob volleys turn into sitting duck overheads that find Bob as the target. When Erik van Dillen and I played together and I was playing really well, I was the captain. But many times when my game went sour, he would take the reins and be more aggressive on the court.

It is common for one team member to get more pumped up than the other and to keep his partner from letting the team down or giving up. On the other hand, sometimes the calm player will keep the emotional player from getting too carried away in arguing a close call or from becoming too upset when things are not going well. It is nice when teammates complement and support each other on the court. Every team has moments that are frustrating and challenging; the great teams are the ones who can overcome those difficult moments and turn the match around.

I have seen partners clash over the issue of captaincy. One memorable example of this happening to professionals is the 1972 Davis Cup match in Romania that Erik van Dillen and I played against Ion Tiriac and Ilie Nastase. Tiriac was the older player and had been the mentor of Nastase, but this match was the turning point when Nastase finally decided to take over the lead. This sudden decision did not sit well with Tiriac. After a few arguments, they stopped communicating altogether. This conflict was painful for Tiriac and Nastase, but it was great fun for us, their worthy opponents, because it made our job easier.

Discuss How You'll Communicate

The doubles teams of today talk quite a bit between points. This can be very helpful, especially for certain types of personalities and during certain situations in a match. The benefit of talking a lot during the match is that you keep each other *in* the match, mentally and emotionally. Without this communication one player might get despondent and make some bad decisions or lose his or her edge.

When Bob and I played Davis Cup and had a captain on the sideline to talk with every other game, we were more effective on the court. I really think that our frequent communication is a big reason we were 12–1 in Davis Cup play. We would talk with the captains and also talk more with each other during the match—partly because we were used to talking with the captain and partly because the captain encouraged us to talk. I think the importance of the occasion also helped us. We were more pumped up for that special opportunity than for normal tournament play.

The more experience players have together, the better they know how their partner is going to react to various situations. Members of great teams know that no matter what happens during the match, their partner is going to fight until the end and try to give them the opportunity to come back.

There are different sorts of communication styles that fit different teams' playing styles. For example, one type is what I call the *cheerleader* style; the partner with this communication style is very vocal and full of positive comments that can be helpful when one player is losing enthusiasm or confidence. My son Trevor played in a collegiate competition that featured a good example of this type of communicator. This cheerleader was playing a match on the court next to my son; he would cheer for his partner after his team's points and cheer for his teammates playing against my son's team in between his team's points. After his match was over, he would cheer from the stands for his buddies who were playing singles. That's the classic team cheerleader personality! Of course, this style can be overused and lose its effect on some teammates. The teammate of such a player may become so accustomed to the cheering that it has no impact; he or she may even become irritated and ask the cheerleader to just be quiet and play the game. Other teammates, though, thrive on this type of continuous hype; it helps them to get emotionally involved and to hit the ball and move even better. This style can also affect the opponents, either annoying them or inspiring them to get more vocal themselves. Many players are intimidated by the cheerleader personality if they can't match the level of intensity.

Another communication style is the *screamer* style. It is similar to the cheerleader style in that both types are vocal, but screamers use their voices to make negative comments. Screamers complain about every close call and all their bad breaks, including let cords (when the ball hits the net and goes over) and bad bounces. They like to point out the fact that the level of play they're exhibiting is the worst tennis they have ever played, and they frequently direct disparaging comments toward their partners and opponents. This personality will self-destruct sooner or later, probably before the match is over. If your partner has screamer tendencies, have a good talk with

Doubles partners must find the style of communication that is most comfortable and most effective for their team. My son Ramsey and I often discuss strategy before a point.

him or her about how to curb them—or walk away from the partnership.

Players who use the *coach* style of communication share strategy ideas and occasionally, on big points, encourage their partner to gear up for the occasion. This style may be helpful for players with a more low-key personality. One concern with this type of communication is that the player being encouraged to gear up may feel pressured, knowing that it must be a big point situation and that he'd better come through for his partner and for the team. The coach style may be more helpful in communicating specific comments on strategy when a change or adjustment is in order.

There are players who do not push each other very much and who don't even talk much about strategy and tactics during the match. I call this the *surgeon* style. Surgeons play straightforward, high-percentage, efficient doubles, without a lot of conversation. Their motto is play quietly, play hard, play smart, and finish the operation cleanly. These players tend to be self-motivators who have confidence in themselves and their teammates. They try to play as hard as they can all the time. A highly competitive opponent could possibly overwhelm this type of team with high intensity if the match gets really close.

One of the great teams of the 1990s, Australians Todd Woodbridge and Mark Woodforde, generally behaved like surgeons on the court, but Todd could get very emotional on occasion. One such occasion was the 1999 Davis Cup final, when they were playing France. The singles matches had been split, so the doubles match (the third match in the best of five series) was the pivotal contest. Todd and Mark had had more success at doubles and held an unbelievable career record, but they had just lost to their Davis Cup opponents, Fabrice Santoro and Olivier Delaitre, in their last two head-to-head matches. Todd started off this match as badly as he could have and lost his serve the first three times he served. He was very upset with himself, and I thought that he had lost it emotionally. The teammates would talk before each serve, and Mark tried to quietly encourage Todd to hang in there. Mark did not get too excited himself; he simply focused on trying to be a calming force on his volatile partner. In this case, the Davis Cup captain, John Newcombe, was also able to talk to his star team when the teams changed sides. John encouraged Todd to keep competing and not be too hard on himself; he told Todd not to try to make the return of serve too good and to be sure of getting the first serve in by taking a little pace off the ball. John also gave Todd some specific strategies to use to think positively and to avoid focusing his attention on how badly he was playing. Todd was trying so hard that he was not allowing himself to play his best. Mark quietly encouraged Todd and conveyed the message that he knew his partner's playing would get better at any moment and that there was no need to dwell on past mistakes. This gave Todd confidence and made it clear to him that, win or lose, they were in it together as a team. Todd finally calmed down, relaxed a little, and began playing like the real Todd Woodbridge. The Aussies finally got it together, and, after being down a set and facing a 5–4 set point, they came back and won quite convincingly in four sets. Australia went on to win the fourth match the next day and to capture the Davis Cup for an impressive 27th time.

So there are different ways to approach team communication. I suggest that you begin your partnership by erring on the side of overcommunication and overencouragement and see how that works. As you play together, you will be able to tell if changes are in order. Evaluate how well your style of communication is working for both partners after a few matches and adjust accordingly.

During the Match

We've discussed the styles of communication that partners can use. Once a team develops its style of communication, the team members can use it to their advantage on the court. There are a number of specific verbal and nonverbal cues that can alter the course of play during a match.

Verbal Cues

Verbal communication has to be positive at all times. Get into the habit of encouraging your partner. These two statements may help you remember to speak in a positive and encouraging manner:

1. Your partner is not missing the ball on purpose.
2. You may miss the same type of shot that your partner just missed, or an even easier shot, on the very next point.

Another important concept to keep in mind is that you are playing as a team and you will win or lose as a team. Neither player can do it alone, and both players will get the credit for the win or the blame for the loss. When you talk to your partner, use the word "we" instead of "you" or "I."

I have, on occasion, heard a player who is playing well say to his partner "just get your return of serve in!" That is the last thing that a player wants to hear when he is not playing his best. It certainly does not help or get him to play better. After playing with someone for a period of time, you will know exactly what type of encouragement helps him or her the most, and your partner will get a better feel for what helps you when you are struggling. For example, Bob Lutz and I played together frequently over a long period of time and therefore didn't talk too much during a match. Erik van Dillen and I, on the other hand, verbally exchanged a lot of encouragement and strategy, and we were more likely to try something a little different, such as an I-formation or both staying back on the return of serve.

I enjoy playing with partners who understand when I am playing badly. They might make a comment, after I miss yet another sitting duck, such as, "No problem, we'll get the next one," or "We can break here," or "We can still win this match." These comments are positive and keep both partners looking toward solid future play rather than reflecting on past mistakes.

I remember the time that Erik van Dillen and I were playing in the quarterfinals of Wimbledon against Dennis Ralston and Arthur Ashe. We really felt that we could win the whole tournament that year. In the match, we were playing OK, but we were not getting any good breaks. I was trying hard and getting extremely frustrated with the situation. After losing another in a series of big points I was about to whine about life being unfair when Erik came close to me and said, "Don't worry, it's only Wimbledon!"

This actually made me laugh, and it suddenly hit me that I had to relax and enjoy the battle rather than getting so uptight that I couldn't see or hit straight. I wish that I could say that we won the match after that; we didn't, but I did play better and have a much better attitude from that point forward.

Communication can be complex. You may say the right thing at the right time, but the way you say it may be all wrong. How many different ways have you heard someone say, "Nice shot"? The same remark can come across as being encouraging, condescending, sarcastic, patronizing, or surprising; it can send any number of messages, depending on the tone in which it is delivered.

If you're playing with someone you know well, you probably know the kind of tone that helps your partner as well as how to get under his or her skin. I have seen this happen often in mixed doubles with husbands and wives. The slightest comment may cause a major confrontation that can not only spoil the match but also endanger the relationship. Make sure that you don't use any tone that could cause a problem. If you have any doubt about whether your statement or tone will have a detrimental effect on your cohort, then keep your mouth closed.

As you are playing a point, there are times when it's important to let your partner know where you are and what you would like him or her to do. For instance, if you are running down a lob that has just gone over your partner's head, your partner should normally cross to the other side of the court to cover the side that you just left. Sometimes it is not obvious who should do what because the ball is nearly down the middle or is being carried by the wind. In such cases, call out where you want your partner to go as you hit the shot. Lobs can be tricky: if you can hit an overhead, your partner should cross and stay at the net; if you cannot hit an offensive shot, your partner needs to cross and move back behind the baseline. So as you go for the ball, yell "cross" or "I got it" when you hit an offensive shot such as an overhead or hard drive. If you're on the run and have to hit a lob, yell "back" so your partner can cross and get behind the baseline to defend.

Some players will call out "you" or "me," which is a pretty efficient and clear system. An experienced team often will know what each partner needs from the other and may not say much, but even veteran teams can get their signals mixed if they don't verbalize their desires as a lob is hit or they are pulled out of position by a great angle shot.

Another situation in which communication is essential is when the ball is hit down the middle, nice and high, and either player could hit it. You should call "mine" or "yours" (or "me" or "you"). Generally the person who calls out first should be in charge, so that a decision is made quickly and with the least amount of confusion.

Nonverbal Cues

Your nonverbal communication on the court is just as important as what you say or how you say it. As with verbal communication, it should be positive rather than negative. Let's say that it is game point, and your partner is returning serve. The opponents miss the first delivery, and you start licking your lips expecting your partner to hammer a great return to enable your twosome to get the much needed break of serve. Your partner gets a juicy one, right to his forehand, and proceeds to hammer it about six feet long or into the middle of the net. You don't say a word, but you roll your eyes to the sky as if you have just witnessed the most egregious crime ever committed by mankind. As if your partner did it on purpose! Now if your partner happens to look at you just as you make this face, he or she will feel very disappointed about letting you down. Your partner may be annoyed by your reaction and get defensive, or may lose whatever confidence has not already been eroded in his or her ability to return serve.

I have sometimes seen a player throw his racket down on the court after his partner has missed a sitter. This is not a subtle gesture, and it can be embarrassing as well as discouraging for the player who missed. This type of reaction, obvious and critical, can be particularly hard on a player's psyche and can hurt the relationship between the partners.

I suggest that you make it a habit to keep both your verbal and nonverbal communication positive so that you don't make the mistake of speaking or acting in a way that you might later regret. The tradeoff is that you can count on each other to help when one of you has a bad day, and you can both stay focused on improving your game instead of dwelling on past mistakes. Remember that the nonverbal cues may need to be practiced, just like the rest of your game. In doubles, communication can be just as important as technique.

The hand signals used by many teams are another important form of on-court communication. Bob Lutz and I sometimes used hand signals during our matches, and so did Erik van Dillen and I.

The key to using hand signals effectively is to keep your opponents guessing what you are going to do while you stay focused on the match. The hand signals in tennis are similar to those between baseball pitchers and catchers. The catcher signals to the pitcher with his bare hand (so he doesn't have to take his glove off) what type of pitch he thinks is best for the situation and then puts his mitt right where he wants the ball to be delivered. The pitcher can shake off the signal by shaking his head, then nod to confirm the signal that indicates the pitch he wants to throw.

In tennis, the net player will give the signal with the nonracket hand behind his or her back to the server (see figure 2.1, *a* and *b*). The signal might indicate only whether or not the net player is going to poach or it might include a suggestion about where the serve should be hit. The server can "shake off" the signal by simply saying no. It is vital that the server acknowledge the final signal before serving to avoid confusion. The server can be as loud as he or she wants in acknowledging the signal because the returning team won't know what the signal is.

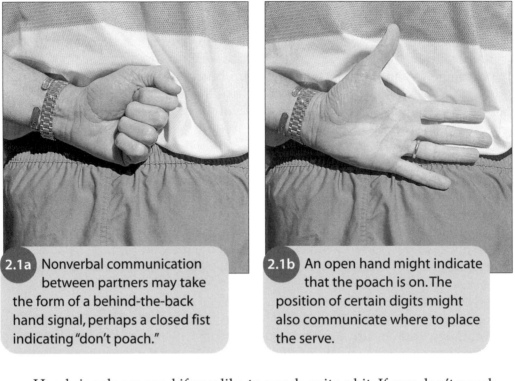

2.1a Nonverbal communication between partners may take the form of a behind-the-back hand signal, perhaps a closed fist indicating "don't poach."

2.1b An open hand might indicate that the poach is on. The position of certain digits might also communicate where to place the serve.

Hand signals are good if you like to poach quite a bit. If you don't poach very often, I think they can be a waste of time. The purpose is for the teammates to communicate and to keep their opponents uncertain as to whether they are going to cross and poach after the serve. There may be a tendency for the player who is returning serve to look at the net player rather than focusing only on the ball. If the returner is looking at the net player with one eye and keeping the other eye on the ball, then there is a good chance that he or she will not make solid contact with the ball.

Another potential problem with hand signals is that fans behind the end of the court could conceivably steal the signals and tip off their team. Of course this would be bad sportsmanship, but it has been known to happen. I will never forget one incident in which the fans behind the court got into the action big time. The United States was playing Spain in Barcelona in the semifinals of the Davis Cup in 1972. The score was one match all going into the doubles. I was playing with Erik van Dillen, and I served throughout this match with the sun at my back. During the second set, every time I served, there would be a quick flash of light in my eyes. I could not understand it at first, but before long I realized that a fan in about the fifth row directly behind the court was reflecting the sun into my eyes as I was serving. That wasn't the signal I wanted to see! I finally went to the chair umpire and asked him to ask the fan to cease and desist. All of the sudden, the umpire could not understand or speak English. The neutral referee said something to the crowd, which didn't seem to help. After a few more points, I decided to take the matter into my own hands. I hit a serve directly into the fifth row. It was a good shot but probably a bad decision because many of the fans started throwing their seat cushions onto the court and booing. About 15 minutes later we resumed the match, and fortunately my "signal" to that particular fan seemed to have put an end to the sun being reflected into my eyes.

Tactical Changes

As you go through the ebb and flow of a match, assess how your original game plan is working and evaluate what changes in tactics should be made. Hopefully you have thought about and talked through some appropriate potential variations in game plan and can integrate new tactics without too much panicked discussion. It is good to have a few options to go to if you are not having success. For instance, if your opponents have big serves and you are not returning them effectively, you may plan to both stay back. Talk through the various difficulties that might occur and how they could be overcome. Practice with these tactical scenarios in mind so that, on the court, you can talk succinctly about how and when to make a change. It is critical that you communicate purposefully and positively during the match so that you can build each other up, discuss possible changes, and play to your full potential.

 # After a Match

After the match is over, good teams critique what happened with a coach, with fellow players, or just with one another. This may occur informally right after the match in the locker room or that night over dinner. Either way, it should be done while the battle is still fresh in your mind. I have found that some teams can remember nearly every point for weeks after an exciting match and others can barely remember whom they played once the last shot is hit. Whatever is the case with you, I recommend that you analyze the pros and cons of your play soon after you have cooled down from the match.

This postmatch analysis will be helpful, especially if you play the same team again. The general concepts discussed can be used as a basis for your next practice session. Be sure to consider the good points as well as the weak points of the match so that you keep the play in perspective. Some teams write these points down in a journal so that they can refer to it if they forget exactly what happened in the match. Use the results of your analysis to fashion drills to improve in your areas of weakness and maybe even in some areas that are already strong. A respected coach once told me that when his players were in a slump, he liked to have them work on their strengths first and then on their weaknesses, in order to help their confidence and keep them feeling more positive.

A cooling down period of a few hours before discussing the match is a particularly good idea if you have just lost a tough, emotional match. The coach and the players can be calmer and more reflective if they've had time to put the match and its contents in perspective. The typical reaction to a close loss is, "we played awful," when in reality only one or two points made the difference. It could quite easily have gone the other way, and you would be celebrating and thinking about how "great you played." Win or lose, it is important to be realistic about how the match went. You might have played well but not converted on two break points and lost, or you might have played badly and won only because the other team played worse.

A good coach can help you and your partner understand exactly what happened and look beyond the obvious result. A coach's input is particularly helpful if he or she has charted the match and can furnish actual statistics on specific areas of play, such as the percentages of first serves made or the number of returns put back in play. These stats don't lie, and the cold, hard facts will clarify what really happened on the field of battle.

Keep the critique of the match factual and not personal. The discussion should revolve around what was or was not done rather than who was to blame. This is not always easy to do, but it is important to speak to the issues and not to the individuals. For instance, when talking about the service game, you might bring up the fact that the first-serve percentage for the team was not as high as it should have been instead of commenting that one player served poorly. You might relate that the intensity level of the team was not consistently high throughout the match and that this enabled the other team to come back.

Go through this assessment of team play systematically so that you don't leave out any area of doubles tennis. Your analysis should include the serve, the return of serve, poaching, positioning, communication, intensity, movement, big-point situations, shot selection, playing conditions, stamina, and mental strengths and weaknesses. You can use the same list of questions you used to evaluate your team's strengths and weaknesses before the match (table 2.1) to guide your postmatch evaluation.

During this analysis you should also talk about what you would do differently the next time. Evaluate your game plan. Again, go through the different areas of the game systematically so that you don't leave out anything. I am sure that some good ideas will come to light as you discuss the match together or with a coach. It may be helpful to write down these ideas so that you don't forget them. Much of what you discuss will also apply to upcoming matches against other teams.

Be sure that the next practice includes work in the weak areas you have identified through your analysis. For instance, if you weren't poaching enough when your partner was serving, do poaching drills with another team or with a coach, and work on when and where to move as you play out some points. Address all the areas that need help based on your evaluation. Use a checklist so that you know you are not missing anything.

Lleyton Hewitt pumps up his team by celebrating a well-placed shot at the 2000 US Open. Winning may be the result of your team's superior play, your opponents' mistakes, or a combination of the two.

Another activity that could prove helpful is to watch the team you lost to play their next match. This can be a bit agonizing because it may bring up some bad memories of your loss, but it can give you ideas about what can be done against that team that you may not have even considered. If you and your partner watch the match together, you can bounce different ideas off each other as far as what might help you against that particular team as well as bits of general strategy. This experience will help you better understand the way your partner thinks, and that in itself will help you as a team.

My final piece of advice about communication after the match, and it is extremely important, is that you should never speak negatively about your partner behind his or her back (or in front of him or her, for that matter). This should be the case in any public setting and even in private unless you are absolutely certain that your conversation is going to remain confidential. Players sometimes speak ill of a partner because they want to blame someone else for a loss. Remember a thought I mentioned earlier: in doubles, you win as a team and you lose as a team. It may make you feel better to let everyone know that it wasn't your fault that the team lost a match, but it certainly is not going to help your partner or your partnership if he or she hears your comments from someone else. Your partner may have played poorly in that match, but you might play as badly or worse in another. If you consistently play better than your partner does, then you probably should look into making a change—but even if this is the case, don't badmouth him or her. Give your partner the benefit of the doubt and keep your comments positive. That is the best way to handle a doubles relationship, both on and off the court.

3

Using Positioning to Play the Percentages

Many of the great teams can hit spectacular shots from all parts of the court. This makes it seem that the matches are won and lost by way of these unusual shots. Having played at different levels of the game from junior player through the pros, I have found that the spectacular shots are crowd pleasers, but they are *not* the ones that win matches on a consistent basis. Great teams can hit the showstoppers, but they win most of their matches by hitting the right shots at the right time. In other words, *they play the percentages.*

It is fun to watch a great team dissect their opponents by using solid, high-percentage shot selection, and then hear the victims complain after the match that the winners didn't do anything special. The losers cannot understand how the other team won. It is much like a chess game. The goal is to stay on the offensive, but there is a time to be conservative and patient, and also a time to be defensive. Each move should be countered with the smartest and highest percentage move by the other team. If your team consistently makes wise decisions, your opponents will probably eventually make a bad decision or be pushed into making a forced error.

I don't get too upset with a player or team that consistently makes good decisions as to what shots to hit but has occasional problems executing those shots. I am more concerned about a player or team that often makes bad decisions about how and where to hit shots and may or may not execute those shots correctly. Let's say that you have hit a return of serve and the server has come to the net and volleyed the ball very deep, so that you must hit your next shot from 10 feet behind the baseline. A smart player decision would be to try to hit a ball low and down the middle or put a high, defensive lob deep and down the middle. Low-percentage, bad decisions for this situation include hitting a short angle shot or blasting a hard, flat ball at one of the opponents.

One team that is particularly good at playing solid, high-percentage doubles is Don Johnson and Jared Palmer, 2001 Wimbledon champions and US Open finalists. They win with smart shot selection, movement around

Players will start in a basic position, but adjust during a point.

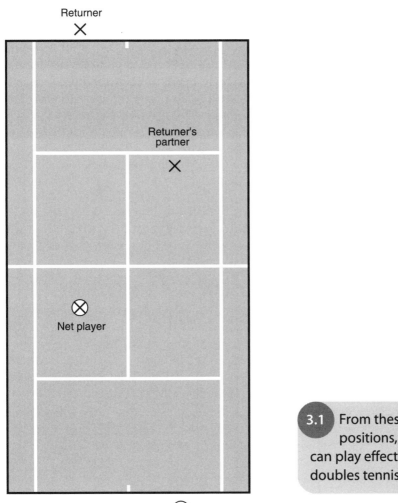

Returner

Returner's partner

Net player

Server

3.1 From these four positions, players can play effective doubles tennis.

the net, and good court positioning. They seldom hit the wrong shot, and they take advantage of their right-handed (Palmer) and left-handed (Johnson) combination to keep their opponents off balance with spin and placement. They use basic court positioning and variations on the basics that I explain in this chapter.

I want to address on-court positioning so that you and your partner will know why you won or, at the very least, be able to determine why you lost. Winning doubles starts with assuming the proper position for each of the four roles you may play on the court before the point begins.

The four basic beginning positions give you something from which to build (see figure 3.1). If you know these basic positions, then you can be effective against most opponents. The main difference in positioning for doubles as opposed to singles is that players need to cover only half the court rather than the whole court. Since the alleys come into play, the doubles court is bigger, but the area for which each player is responsible is smaller. In the next two chapters, I will go through some variations on these basic positions that you can use to keep opponents with unusual strengths and weaknesses off balance. These starting positions are meant to give you the best opportunity to play good, high-percentage tennis.

 Server

As the server you are the dictator; the other players have to react to your actions. Some servers forget this simple concept and do not take advantage of being in command. Because the server starts the point, he or she sets the

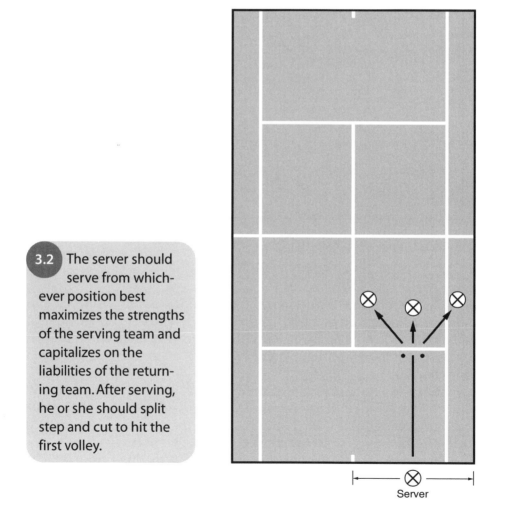

3.2 The server should serve from whichever position best maximizes the strengths of the serving team and capitalizes on the liabilities of the returning team. After serving, he or she should split step and cut to hit the first volley.

Server

pace, within reason, and serves when ready. Stand about halfway between the center service line and the outside sideline so that you can serve with equal ease to either the forehand or the backhand of the opponent. You can stand anywhere along the baseline to serve, all the way into the alley, if appropriate (see figure 3.2).

The serving position may not be the same for every serve of every match. It really depends on the strengths of both the server and returner. If a server has trouble getting the serve to the backhand consistently (on the deuce side), he or she can move closer to the center. If a server is not effectively serving wide, he or she can move toward or into the alley.

The serving stance itself will vary ever so slightly as the server moves toward the sideline; otherwise the server would be too open or too closed, depending on which court he or she is serving to. For example, if you are right-handed and are serving to the deuce court, your stance will become more closed as you move toward the sideline because more of your back will be facing the court into which you are serving (see figure 3.3*a*). As you move away from the center you should angle your front foot, hips, and shoulders slightly so that your body is in the same position in relation to the target on all serves (see figure 3.3*b*).

3.3a As the target area for the serve changes, the server's body must shift. This position is too closed for serving to the deuce court.

3.3b This is the proper stance for serving to the deuce court. Note the alignment of the front foot, hips, and shoulders.

A change in position will keep your opponent off balance because it means the angle at which the ball arrives at the returner will be slightly different. In this sense, a tennis server has an edge over a baseball pitcher: a pitcher always has to throw from the mound, whereas a server can alter his or her position and therefore the returner's perspective on the serve. Servers should take advantage of this opportunity by varying their position along the baseline.

The most common error I see the average server make is standing too close to the center, so that he or she is not able to serve wide and cover the wide return of serve effectively. Standing close to the center enables you to serve down the center well, but it limits your serving options and therefore makes it easier for your opponent to field your delivery. Also, this position does not allow you to open up the court well. If you do serve wide while standing close to the center, then your opponent will be able to return the serve away from you and send you off court chasing the ball, whether you serve and volley or serve and stay back.

Net Player

The server's partner, or net player, plays an important role in supporting the team goal of holding serve (winning the game during which you are serving). Many people think that the server is mainly or entirely responsible for winning the game in which he or she is serving. Sometimes the opposite is true, when the net player is so active that he or she intimidates the player returning the serve.

The player at the net should generally stand about halfway between the net and the service line, and halfway between the center service line and the outside alley line (see figure 3.4). That player's role is to keep the player who is returning serve uncomfortable by being very active. Moving and changing positions often causes the service returner to spend more time thinking about the net player than the ball.

The net player's position and attitude both affect the return of serve player. If the net player looks unprepared or lacking in intensity, then the returner will be more relaxed. But if the net player looks agile, mobile, and aggressive, then the returner will feel pressured and less confident about returning the serve because of the threat of the net player crossing.

The most common error I see net players make is standing too close to the net. I have even heard some teaching pros say that net players should stand close enough to the net to reach out with their racket and touch the net. I disagree with this advice for two reasons. First, it is obvious that a player who is close to the net is vulnerable to the lob. Second, ask yourself, is it easier to move forward or backward? Everyone I have asked says it is easier to move forward. Since this is the case, it makes sense then to position

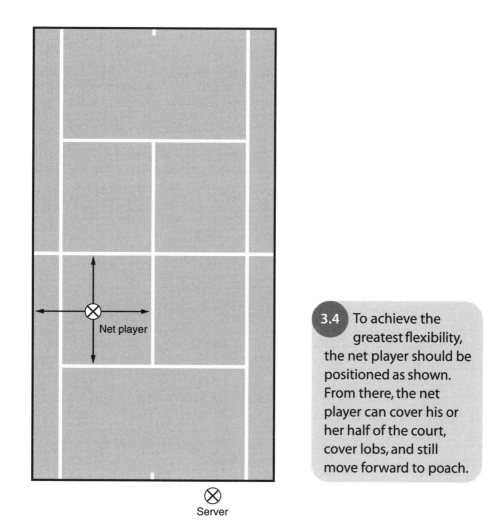

Net player

3.4 To achieve the greatest flexibility, the net player should be positioned as shown. From there, the net player can cover his or her half of the court, cover lobs, and still move forward to poach.

Server

yourself halfway between the net and the service line rather than too close to the net. If you start a little further back, then you have a better chance to cover the lob. I feel that you should try to cover your own lobs whenever possible, and not rely on your partner to cover every ball that has the potential to go over your head. Your partner has enough to do to cover his or her own half of the court. Now if you do stand halfway between the service line and the net, and a ball is hit short, you can move forward with a few quick steps. If you are alert, then you will not often get hurt by the short ball, and you will be able to cover most of the lobs hit on your side of the court.

The other mistake I see, particularly in mixed doubles, is the server's partner standing too close to the alley or even in the alley. This is usually done because the macho male partner thinks that he is so much better, quicker, stronger, faster, and who knows what else than his female partner that he can cover every ball except those hit in her alley. He may say something like, "just cover your alley, sweetheart," and put her three feet from the net. With the server's partner so far from the center of the court, the returner has a big space into which to return the serve. The threat of the net player doing anything is all but gone. Seeing the big opening makes the returner feel less threatened and more relaxed, and therefore he or she is better able to hit a high percentage of good cross-court returns of serve. This can spell death for the serving team (and sometimes for the relationship), and it is no fun for the female player.

If, however, the net player stands a few feet from the center line, the down-the-line return becomes more tempting and the cross-court return area becomes really small. From a returner's point of view, seeing the feet of the net player closer to the center diminishes the returner's confidence in successfully getting the ball cross court without interception. If the returner is not comfortable hitting the return of serve down the line, then this position can be quite effective. I would suggest that you stay in this position until the returner shows that he or she can hurt you down the line. At the US Open Final in 2001, Palmer and Johnson were quite effective with Johnson serving his lefty serve and Palmer very close to the middle of the court. They ended up cutting off many of the returns with a volley. The opposing team just wasn't able to return down the line well early in the match. Unfortunately for Palmer and Johnson, they lost to the South African pair of Wayne Black and Kevin Ullyett, who eventually adjusted and hit some good returns down the line.

The net player has to be involved in the match and carry his or her own weight or the team will not be successful. Positioning for the first and second serves may vary slightly. Generally, on the first serve, the net player can stand a little closer to the net because the returner is not likely to return as effectively. The net player will probably have more opportunities to help the server by intercepting the weaker returns of serve. When standing closer on the first serve, the net player's primary concern is to be prepared for the possible lob.

On a second serve, the net player may want to move back a step so that he or she has a split second more time to defend a ball that is hit at him or her. Also, the net player is less likely to poach on the second serve because the returner will be more aggressive. This reinforces the importance of the doubles concept of getting a high percentage of first serves in the court. These are general positioning guidelines; as the match progresses a good serving team will implement subtle changes and variations to keep their opponents off balance and guessing. I will explain these options in chapter 4.

Returner

The server's position and the types of serve that he or she normally hits help determine the service returner's position. The particular strengths and weaknesses of the service returner also play a role.

Basically, the returner should stand so that he or she has an equal opportunity to return any ball hit by the server. Another way to say this is that the returner should stand in a position that bisects the angle of the range of potential serves (see figure 3.5, *a* through *c*). For example, if the server stands close to the center service line to deliver the ball, then the returner should stand where he or she would stand to return a serve in singles, that is, about halfway between the center line and the singles sideline. The more the server moves toward the sideline to begin the point, the more the returner should move away from the center of the court to prepare for the return.

The main goal of the returner is to get the ball back, especially on the big first serve, and to make the serving team hit another ball. The biggest mistake I see returners make is to stay in a certain spot on the baseline for every serve. If the server is punishing an opponent with a certain serve, such as the wide

Returner

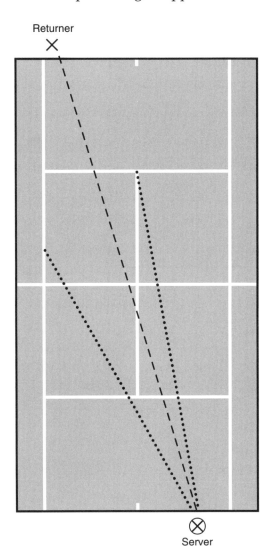

Server

3.5a In determining the position that splits the area in which the server is most likely to hit the ball, the returner should allow for the fact that the net is lower in the middle of the court (3.0 feet versus 3.3 feet at the sides).

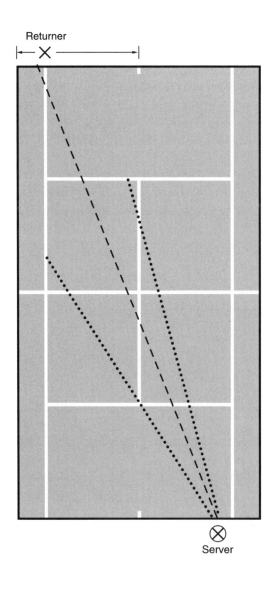

Returner

Server

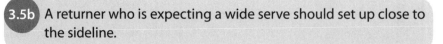

3.5b A returner who is expecting a wide serve should set up close to the sideline.

Returner
X

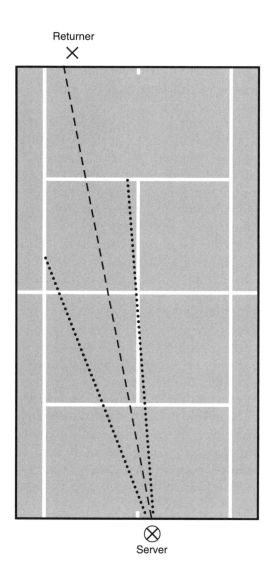

$\otimes$
Server

3.5c The returner should be aware of a server's preferences and make adjustments for any shifts in serving position. If the server stands close the center, the returner should set up as he or she would in a singles match.

serve, and the returner doesn't make an adjustment, then the returner is unaware of the server's strengths or serving position. I have seen players who never made an adjustment during the match, such as standing closer to the sideline to receive the victimizing shot, walk off the court talking about getting killed by the wide serve.

There are two basic returning positions, one for returning a first serve and another for returning the second serve. Generally a team will serve a harder, flatter first serve, which can be very difficult to return if it goes in.

Since the main goal in returning the first serve is to get the ball back over the net, one very helpful adjustment you can make is to move further back to give yourself a little more time to get a read on the ball. It is still surprising to me, even after all these years, how beneficial it is for the returner to move just three to five feet further back from the server. You'll find that the split second you gain can make a big difference in your return. And getting one or two more returns back in play just might be the factor that allows you the opportunity to break serve. Besides giving you more time to react, moving back gives the server a different perspective. When you stand back further to return, it makes the service box seem longer because the server's perspective is determined by the net, the service line, the baseline, and the returner's position. Obviously the net height and two lines do not change (if the net is measured before the match) but the returner's presence affects the server's visual assessment of the court. If the returner stands way back, the service box will seem longer, resulting in the server's tendency to serve long. If the returner stands closer to the net, the server will see the service box as shorter and therefore may hit more serves into the net. In sum, the basic forward or back position of the returner on the first serve will depend on the strength of the serve. Generally, the harder the serve, the further back the returner should play.

On the second serve, the returner's position should change according to his or her mind-set. He or she may move forward and to the side, thereby gaining a better opportunity to hit his or her strongest shot. This is a chance to take advantage of the opponent's weaker delivery. The returner's mind-set should shift from reacting on the first serve to dictating the point on the second serve. With really good servers, the second serve may still be formidable, but it is fairly certain that it will be weaker than the first serve. I like to take some chances on the second serve and let my opponents know that if they miss their first serve, they will have to pay the price. Over the length of a match, the server will do one of three things: concentrate better and serve more first serves in while maintaining the same pace, keep missing and giving me opportunities to return the serve, or take off some pace on the first serve to get a higher percentage in. The latter two of these adjustments will make the job of returning serve easier.

The returner's choice of position can have a big impact on the match. Use position to plant the seed of doubt in the server's mind as to what you might be trying to do on the return.

Martina Hingis–Anna Kournikova

Martina Hingis is the most well-rounded women's player that I have seen play. She has all the shots and is a great tactician on the court. She can figure out an opponent's game fairly quickly, and she has the tools to put into action a successful game plan. The only area in which she is weak is her serve. Some of the top women are able to take advantage of the second serve in particular and put Martina on her heels with their return of serve. She has often partnered with Anna Kournikova, and together the women have become an outstanding doubles team whose popularity has helped to fill stadiums around the world.

Both women have good returns of serve that frequently put their opponents on the defensive early in the point. They are also quite active at the net; when an opponent hits an effective return of serve they will often poach and knock off their foe's weak shot. They have quick hands, and they make impressive reflex volleys that keep them in the point. Another strong aspect of their game is their ability to hit angles that take their opponents off the court. This ability produces some interesting tennis and makes them fun to watch.

Tactically, both Martina and Anna have a very good feel for determining the right shot to attempt in every situation. Of course they do not make every shot, but their decisions about which shot to try are usually right on the money. I have seen them turn around a point in which they were in a defensive position by hitting the smart shot and taking control of the situation. They sometimes serve and stay back; this is unorthodox positioning, but their control of their groundstrokes and their ability to come to the net when the opportunity presents itself enables them to win many points.

Most of the time these women make it clear that they enjoy playing with each other by actively supporting each other before and after points. You sometimes feel that they are trying hard to please one another or, at least, not to let each other down. This is a great attitude to have toward your partner, and for a lot of players, feeling that you are in it together keeps the experience fun. Like the other great teams that have played the game, Martina and Anna hate to lose and push themselves to play harder when the going gets tough.

Returner's Partner

The returner's partner is in the hot seat. If the returner hits a good return, the partner should be in a position to take advantage of it. If the return is not hit well, then the partner is in a position to get killed. The returner's partner must be alert and ready to go forward or back.

The first job of this player is to call the service line. The returner's partner is in perfect position to call the ball, and this takes some pressure off the player returning the serve. This way, all the returner has to think about is calling the center service line and sideline and, of course, hitting the serve back.

To call the service line, stand near the service line, facing forward toward the net, and turn your head toward the line. Watch the ball all the way until it lands, if it looks like it is going to be close (see figure 3.6a). If it appears that the serve is not going to land close to the line, and it is way in, then you should immediately direct your attention to the net player on the other side of the net (see figure 3.6b). That player is the one who can hurt you first. If you focus on the net player, you will have a better chance to react to a potential poach.

3.6a The returner's partner should monitor and call close serves.

3.6b If the ball is clearly in, the returner's partner should anticipate and prepare for the actions of the opposing net player.

Some good players advocate looking at the returner as he or she hits the ball and then following the ball off the returner's racket. I don't like this system. If the net player poaches, you won't have enough time to react to the ball; you will need to turn your head back toward the other side of the net, and you won't pick up the net player's move as quickly (see figure 3.7).

Another common mistake in calling the serve is facing the line (like a linesman) to make the call. That works well enough for calling the serve, but then you have to turn your whole body back toward the net to play. If your opponents poach, you probably will not be ready in time to respond.

The starting position for the returner's partner should be halfway between the centerline and the outside alley line, and near the service line. A couple of variables affect whether the partner should be inside the service line or behind it a couple of steps. The quality of the serve is the first element to consider. If the opponent is serving particularly well, then the returner should stand back a little on the first serve and the returner's partner should do the same. This gives both the returner and his or her partner a split second more time to react to the ball. Another critical variable is the consistency of the service returns. If the returner is having problems returning the serve, then the partner needs to move back.

One of my Davis Cup partners, Erik van Dillen, was extremely good at being flexible in his positioning and movements when I was returning serve. One of his moves that I remember well was effective when I would hit a poor return that turned out to be a sitter for the other net player. Instead of standing there at the mercy of the player who was crossing and looking to give him a little attention, Erik would backpedal while keeping his eye on the opposing volleyer and keeping his racket out in front of him (see figure 3.8). This gave him time to get his racket on the ball, if possible, and poke it back

3.7 Turning to watch the returner hit the ball uses time that could be better spent tracking the net player.

into play. Also, opponents would end up hitting the volley too hard or too deep because of the moving target.

Normally after the first serve, the returner will move forward and think offensively; that means the chance of both players taking advantage of a good return is enhanced. So in a second serve situation, the returner's partner should move inside of the service line and be ready to poach.

The most common fault I see in this position is passivity. I think that sometimes the player who is not directly involved in hitting the ball feels that he or she does not have to pay attention until after the return of serve is hit. It can be quite an eye-opener for such players to watch the pros play. All four players are intensely focused every time the ball goes into play, thinking about how they can help their team. The ready position used by the pros, whether they are returning the ball or not, is always the same. Their feet are about shoulder-width apart or a little wider, and their knees are slightly bent.

3.8 Moving with the racket in front of the body while watching the opposing volleyer gives the returner's partner the best possible chance to get into position for the next shot.

They are on their toes, poised to move forward, waist slightly bent, very much like a basketball player guarding an opponent. They hold their rackets out in front of them, using their nondominant hand to support the frame at the throat. They stare intensely at the rival who is hitting the ball, and they expect every ball to come to them. Look into their eyes, and you can see that they are *into* the match.

These great players make seemingly impossible gets. This is the result of preparation, expecting the ball to fly their way, keen anticipation, quick recovery, and, in some cases, educated guessing. It is beautiful to watch reflex volleys come back, but it is even more fun to actually participate in fast and furious exchanges. High-quality play starts with good positioning, including a proper ready position.

4

Maximizing Your Serve

A very high percentage of points are awarded within the first two hits of the ball, the serve and the return of serve. For this reason it is vital to concentrate on what you can do to maximize the serve and to counter with an effective return of serve. In chapter 3, I emphasized the importance of being in control of the point when you are serving. The serve should be a big weapon even if it is not of high velocity. In doubles your partner can help make your serve a better weapon by helping to keep your opponents off balance.

In chapter 3, I outlined the basic positions in which each player should stand to begin a match and talked about making some changes to those positions, if necessary, to get the momentum going your way. In this chapter,

I deal with the specific modifications the serving team—the server and net player—can make. In chapter 5, I'll cover some adjustments the receiving team—the returner of the serve and his or her partner—can implement. Remember, the goal is to keep your opponents uncomfortable and uncertain about what you might or might not do. You have the advantage in doubles of having two players to impact your adversaries on the opposite side of the net. Now, you don't need to jump up and down and shout at your opponents to intimidate them. Your position and the subtle adjustments you make as the point begins will make a very strong statement.

 Server

Being on the serving side should give your team a sense of power; you are in position to score. As you start each point with your partner at the net, be aware that you're likely to win games in which your team is serving or holding serve. The goal is to prevent a service break by the other team. In this sport, you get a second chance if you miss a first serve—take advantage of that fact. Having said that, I am going to relate ways to make the most of both the first and second serves.

If you are struggling with your serve, use the following checklist to assess your mechanics (table 4.1). Evaluate your toss (height, forward, and sideward positions), stance, arm position, wrist position, head position, and weight distribution.

First Serve

Before I talk about some key things you can do to become a more effective server, I want to note what I think is perhaps the most fundamental concept in serving in doubles tennis: Strive to get a high percentage of first serves into the service box. The reason that this is a cornerstone of great doubles is that a well-placed first serve allows your team to stay in charge of the game. The server is in charge when he or she steps up to the line to hit the first serve. If he or she misses the first serve, the player returning the second serve suddenly feels on equal or better footing with the server and will now look to attack. A missed first serve takes away the serving team's sense of being in control and gives the returning team a great boost. Before you hit the first serve, your opponents don't *know* if you are going to send it at 120 miles per hour or 50 miles per hour, and their uncertainty works to your advantage. The speed of the first serve you deliver doesn't matter all that much. But your opponents know that if you miss the first serve you will reduce the pace of your second serve dramatically in order to avoid double-faulting. If you can execute a high percentage of good first serves (even at less than top speed) from a variety of positions, with an assortment of spins, and with accurate

Table 4.1
Serving Evaluation Checklist

Serve segment	What to check for
Initial stance	Feet at about 45-degree angle to the baseline and parallel to one another Slightly forward weight distribution Upright and relaxed posture Arms relaxed and positioned in front of body at about stomach level
Backswing	Racket falls straight down, back, and up to back-scratching position Synchronized arm movements
Shoulder turn	A sideways, coiled position is established
Toss technique	Ball is held in the last two digits of the hand in a sideways position Arm moves slowly and stays straight
Head position	Head follows the toss up, remains up to watch contact
Weight transfer	Body weight shifts to back foot as racket moves Knees bend Movement up and forward toward contact
Tempo	Acceleration into the shot as contact point is reached
Contact point	Racket arm is fully extended Forward or backward contact so that ball bounces just inside the baseline Contact occurs, from the side view, at about 1 o'clock for first serve and 12 o'clock for second
Followthrough	Racket continues moving toward target with arm pronation

placement, then the returning team will have to do something special, or perhaps something desperate, to break serve.

I get a kick out of watching big, macho club players hitting the first serve at 120 miles an hour into the back fence 90 percent of the time and then having to resort to a little 20-mile-an-hour dink of a second serve. These players look good for the instant they hit the big first serve, but they are soon chewed up by friendly adversaries who can't wait to get a racket on that marshmallow second delivery. Some of these guys can't understand how they can lose to "substandard" foes despite their ability to hit the first serve so much harder. Many times these beasts have nothing else in their repertoire of strokes; they bludgeon the ball on every occasion. A little knowledge and finesse can help

Experienced, accomplished servers, such as Arantxa Sanchez-Vicario, understand the value of a well-placed first serve.

a player like this to become a more effective competitor. Mixing up the big shots with some spins, angles, and steady shots makes the forceful shots even better. It is much like a baseball pitcher throwing some curves, some sliders, and some change-ups; the batter doesn't know what to expect and therefore is kept off balance.

I mentioned in chapter 2 the match Bob Lutz and I played against the great team of Frew McMillan and Bob Hewitt. They had very average, if not below average, speed on their first serves. At first blush, you might even think that their serves had so little speed they couldn't possibly be a world-class team. Upon closer inspection, on the same court and across the net from McMillan and Hewitt, you would find that it was darn difficult to break serve against them. Why? They would get in very accurate first serves, keeping you a little off balance with accurate shot variety and placement, and get to the net quickly. Unless you hit an exceptional return, they would nail the volley so that you would have to resort to a low-percentage shot to try to win the point. They would not let you get a look at too many second serves, and they would just not miss a volley. After playing them once, you would likely walk off the court talking to yourself about how badly you returned serve and how you would surely get them next time. After playing them again, you would finally realize that these guys were the real thing and that you would have to raise the level of your game to have a chance of beating them.

Second Serve

The key element that determines whether a player is considered a good server is how well he or she hits the *second* serve. That is, your serve is only as good as your second serve. Being a good server means that when you really need to hit a deep, accurate, heavily spun ball with enough pace, you are able to do so most of the time, even under the pressure of a second serve. Anybody can flail wildly at the first serve and get it in occasionally, then push the second serve in. I would rather play against someone with a huge first serve and a weak second serve than a player with an average first serve and a great second serve. Players with a great second serve usually possess such solid mechanics that they also have a very good first serve. One such player is Pete Sampras, who has one of the greatest first serves as well as one of the best second serves of all time. When he plays doubles he knows that if he misses the first serve, his second serve will still be hard to handle. He has come through with a great second serve in big-point situations so many times that people kind of expect him to do so.

The second serve is generally hit with more spin, to control the ball and to keep it in the court. It takes practice to get a feel for how hard you can hit the second serve and not miss the court. Be very clear in your mind as to your optimal pace and trajectory for your consistent second serve.

When you are hitting the second serve, keep in mind that you are still in control of the point and therefore don't need to be too conservative. If you are double-faulting too much, throttle back the pace or put more spin on the ball. The second serve can become a problem if you lose confidence. If you doubt your ability to hit it well, you will begin to feel tense. The more you tense you get, the less likely you are to have good rhythm and technique. When you feel yourself getting tense, try relaxing your grip on the racquet and making sure the toss is accurate. Remember, you do not have to hit every toss. I have seen McEnroe catch tosses on the center court of Wimbledon because they weren't just right.

A good way to practice is to play with only one serve. This forces you to concentrate on every serve and makes you aware of how much power and how much spin you should put into your serve.

If you are still unable to identify and correct your serving problems, see your local tennis professional for guidance.

Keep Your Opponents Guessing

If your opponents don't know what to expect from you, they will have a hard time being adequately prepared. There are four ways to keep your opponents guessing. You can adjust your positioning, type of serve, placement, and pace. There are many variations within each of these four areas that you can use to keep your opponents wondering what is coming next.

Positioning

When serving, vary your *positioning* on the baseline so that the ball continually approaches the opponent from a different angle. To do this well, you must practice serving from different locations. Three issues about the starting position are especially important:

1. **Delivering the ball from different spots on the baseline** (see figure 4.1, next page) **really does keep the opposition off balance.** Players tend to have a hard time getting into a groove when the serves they are attempting to return originate from unexpected locations. It is particularly disturbing to them to have the ball come toward their body from a different angle.

2. **By varying your positioning, you are trying to make your opponents uncomfortable, but if you don't practice serving from different locations, *you* will feel uncomfortable.** I am sometimes not able to serve confidently from a certain spot that is only a few feet from my favorite serving location. I therefore practice specifically from three or four points on the baseline, until I feel comfortable and capable of delivering the type of serve I'd want to use in a tight situation from each position. If you give up the advantage of being comfortable, then you are defeating the purpose of varying your position.

Returner
X

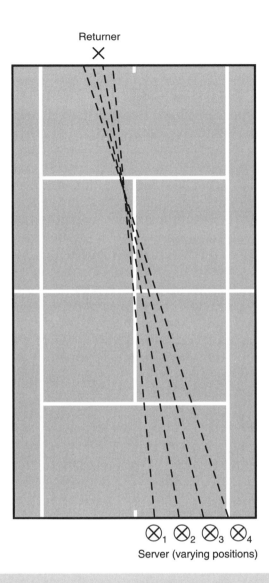

$\otimes_1$ $\otimes_2$ $\otimes_3$ $\otimes_4$
Server (varying positions)

4.1 A server can place the ball in roughly the same location from different positions. When the balls come in from different angles, the returner is forced to make an adjustment.

3. **Set up your adversary so that on a big point you can hit the serve from whatever location on the baseline that player has the most difficulty dealing with.** By moving around you will keep your opponent unsure of what to expect and also become familiar with his or her weaknesses in the return of serve. Then when you *really* need a point, you can go with your best against his or her worst.

Type of Serve

Consider varying the *type* of serve you hit; this in turn involves considering the *spin* you put on the ball. Some players always hit the same type of serve with the same amount of spin on the ball. This is well and good, if by so doing you are able to win your service games handily. But better players will adjust to the serve and start returning it more effectively. The trick, as with your serving positioning along the baseline, is to vary what you do in order to keep your opponents guessing and to keep you in command.

There are three basic types of serves: flat, slice, and topspin (see table 4.2). Each results in a different bounce on the court and elicits a different reaction from your opponents. Before the match, be sure to discuss with your partner, coach, and other involved parties how your opponents are likely to react to each type of serve. It would be a crime to play a match and then find out that you served your opponent's favorite serve every single time. Even the pros have a favorite serve that they would prefer to receive if they were given a choice. I suggest that you don't do your opponents the favor of catering to their wishes; instead, make them hit the type of serve they like the least.

Bob Lutz and I have played some matches where we had to be careful about serving certain serves because our opponents would eat them up as

Table 4.2

The Three Basic Serves

Type of serve	How to hit it	Consequences
Flat	Contact with racket face flat toward target Hit directly behind ball Swing harder for more speed Swing straight forward	Hits and bounces straight through the court
Slice	Contact with racket face at angle to target Hit right side of ball* Swing harder for more spin	Bounces low and to the left* Spins off court on the deuce side* Swing across ball from left to right*
Topspin	Contact with racket face at angle to target Hit the lower left side of ball* Swing harder for more kick Swing up and from left to right*	Bounces high and to the right * Goes off court on the ad side*

* Serving how-tos and consequences are written for right-handed servers. Left-handed servers should change each item marked with this symbol to the opposite side (i.e., "bounces high and to the right" for a right-handed server would read "bounces high and to the left" for a left-handed server).

they would a tasty dessert. On the day we played Peter Fleming and John McEnroe in the final of the 1980 US Open, Peter was having an easy time with our flat serves to his backhand but was struggling with topspin or slice serves to his backhand and with slice serves to his forehand. We therefore hit the majority of our serves to these two locations and used the slice serve into the body; this proved very effective. If we had continued going flat down the middle to his backhand, he would have hurt us badly.

Once you realize that you have the option of hitting these three types of serves, you must ask yourself whether or not *you can hit* all three serves effectively. As with serving from different areas on the baseline, it takes practice to be able to hit each type of serve well and confidently in a big match. Make sure that you understand the mechanics, and practice each delivery until you feel that you would be comfortable executing it under pressure. It would be unfortunate to know that you should hit a particular type of serve on a big point but not be sure that you could pull it off. In chapter 7, I'll provide some drills that will enable you to become a more successful server.

In general, the best grip for all types of serves is a continental grip (see figure 4.2*a*). There are two schools of thought as to how to teach proper grip for the serve. One is to start beginners with an Eastern grip (figure 4.2*b*) and then, as they get older, stronger, or better, have them move the hand more to the left to assume the continental grip. The other is to simply start learning the serve with the continental grip. I have gone back and forth on this issue but I feel that it is best to start and stay with the continental grip. This allows a player to hit the flat serve with the pronation of the arm and also to hit the slice or topspin.

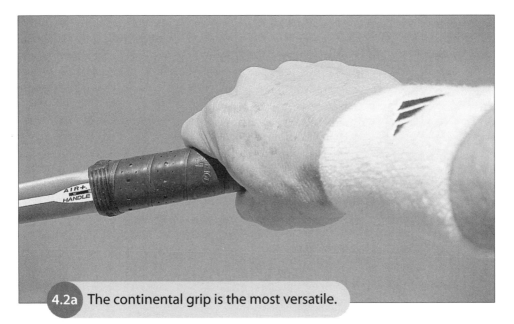

4.2a The continental grip is the most versatile.

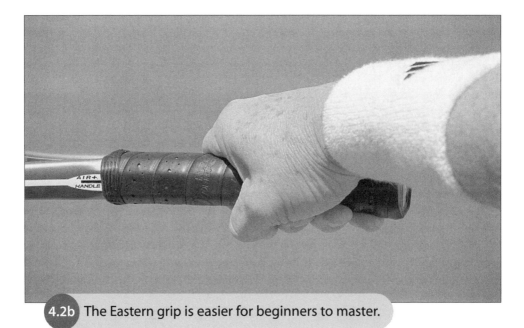

4.2b The Eastern grip is easier for beginners to master.

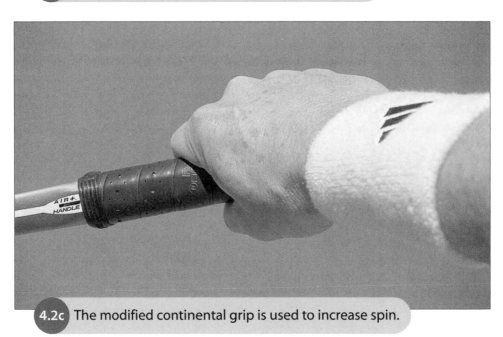

4.2c The modified continental grip is used to increase spin.

To hit the ball with more spin, the grip can be moved a little more to the left; this allows the hand to more easily produce a glancing blow across the ball (see figure 4.2*c*).

Flat Serve

The hard, flat serve is the big weapon. It is also the most difficult to get in on a consistent basis. If it doesn't go in, you are left in the vulnerable position of having to do whatever it takes to put the second serve in the court. Today many top junior, college, and professional players frequently go for the hard, flat first serve, and they often wind up in trouble because they miss. I think that you can hit the flat first serve in doubles *if* you take a little pace off the shot and hit it accurately into the corners (see figure 4.3, *a* and *b*). This will put a higher percentage of serves in and make things tough on your opponents.

4.3a The flat serve must not be hit so hard that accuracy of placement suffers. It can be executed, as shown here, by hitting right behind the ball while leaning into the court.

4.3b A flat serve into the corner is tough to handle, even for good returners.

Some tennis players love to return a ball that is hit flat, even if it is hit fairly hard. These players use the pace their opponents put on the ball; they block the ball at the feet of the net rushing server, and hit it firm and deep toward the baseline if the server stays back. Players like this seem invincible because they return this type of serve so well. They may, on the other hand, be unable to return a serve that has more spin than pace and that bounces quite high. Faced with that type of serve, their seeming invincibility may suddenly be replaced by vulnerability. It is amazing to watch the confidence of such a player drop and to see a mere mortal again on the other side of the net.

Slice or "Slider"

With so many players using a semi-Western grip or full Western grip for the forehand, the wide slice serve is particularly effective (see figure 4.4, *a* and *b*). This serve is difficult for the returner to handle because it slides away and stays low after it hits the ground. It often produces outright errors or mis-hit shots that can go anywhere. Hitting wide sets up a great one-two combination because it opens up the center of the court for your next shot. It is important to tell your partner when you plan to hit the "slider," so that he or she can be ready to move toward the alley a little to cover a possible return

4.4a The wide slice serve is a good option for players who favor the Western grip for the forehand.

4.4b Returners have great difficulty keeping up with a slider that bounces away.

4.4c A slider that moves in on the returner presents a different set of challenges.

down the line. If the wide, slice serve is not hit as well as the server had hoped or if the returner has anticipated it, then the net player has to be alert for the shot down the line. The down-the-line shot is shortest and takes the least amount of time to get by the net player, so that is the first shot to cover.

The other way to use the slider is to hit it so that it moves into the returner's body, cramping his or her ability to move (see figure 4.4c). This is a particularly difficult serve to return with the backhand; the situation is similar to that of a baseball batter fighting off an inside curveball. The returner is unlikely to get off a good solid shot.

The slice or slider serve is executed by hitting the ball with a glancing blow that imparts sidespin. The ball picks up sidespin because the racket is facing the target as the ball leaves the racket, but the path of the racket is slightly to the side. The feeling is that you are swinging around the outside of the ball, with the hand cupping the ball (turning inward), led by the little finger. In reality, as soon as you make contact with the ball, the arm pronates (palm turns downward), with the thumb leading the turning of the hand. The feeling is what you should focus on; the reality will take care of itself. The sound of the slice is a soft whooshing or whipping sound rather than the solid pop of the flat serve.

Topspin

The topspin or kick serve is the serve of choice for most good players because it dips down after going over the net. This shot can clear the net by quite a bit and still go into the service box. It can also be hit with various degrees of sidespin, which will not only cause it to bounce high but also to veer off to the right (for right-handed players, to the left for lefties) after it bounces. This gives the opponent a high ball to handle and also forces him or her to reach out with a backhand to make contact. This is a difficult serve for players with one-handed or two-handed backhands to return.

Most players actually hit the first serve with a little topspin to help it come down safely into the servie box after going over the net. It is a good idea to practice using different amounts of spin, so that you can apply the appropriate amount with confidence during a big-point, second-serve situation. Make a conscious effort to hit a few with just a little spin, some with more spin, and some with a great deal of spin. Have another player or a coach try to determine the amount of spin.

The topspin serve (the American twist is the extreme version of the topspin serve) is hit by brushing the racket up and across the back of the ball, from left to right for right-handed players and from right to left for lefties. The legs need to bend and spring up to put more upward thrust into the ball. The toss should be back and a little to the left, in order to allow you to get a good grip on the ball. It is important to swing hard, which is not a natural inclination when you are trying to get control. By swinging hard and brushing the ball forcefully, you will get more spin and therefore more control. This spin causes the ball to take more of an arc over the net and to kick up—away from the backhand of a right-hander (see figure 4.5a) or up and in toward the body on a forehand (see figure 4.5b)—when it bounces. If the ball is being brushed properly, you should be able to hear a whooshing or whipping sound, rather than a popping sound, at contact. Many players struggle to execute this serve correctly.

Placement

The third element that will give you an opportunity to keep your opponents off balance is *placement*. It may seem obvious that you'd want to hit the ball into the corners so that your opponents can't get a racket on the ball. That would be ideal, but, in tennis as in life, the ideal is often difficult to achieve.

While you are warming up for your match, determine which shot is the weakest shot in the repertoire of each of your opponents so that when you really have your back against the wall, you will know how and where to serve. Once you determine each opponent's weakest shot, you will know what position and type of serve is likely to be most effective against him or her.

When playing a smaller player who does not have much reach, the serve into the corner is a very smart serve to use. Your opponent will be continually lunging to get the ball back. If you vary the corners, the player will not know which way to go and will always be on the stretch.

Against certain opponents, the serve into the corner may backfire if you don't hit it just right. A tall, rangy player likes to see the ball out away from the body; serving toward the corners might put the ball right in his or her strike zone if you don't hit it precisely where you want it. This will enable the player to swing away with fluidity and power. The serve that is more effective against this type of player is one that goes in toward the body. This cramps the player's swing and forces him or her to push the return back instead of taking a free swing at the ball. I know this feeling because it has frustrated me over the years (please don't tell any of my buddies—the less observant ones who haven't figured this out yet will have an edge on me the next time we play).

You can hit the ball into the body with a flat, kick, or slice serve. It is very difficult for a returner to handle this kind of serve without knowing the direction it will come from or the type of spin it will have. I know some players who can handle a serve into the body that is flat, but they get really confused and can't generate any power when a serve comes in at slower pace and with a great deal of spin.

Pace

Making use of positioning, spin, and placement, and the options within those areas allows you to continually present a different serve to your opponents. There is another element that can further increase your options. That is *pace*.

4.5a Returners struggle to make contact with the topspin serve. It kicks up and away from the backhand.

4.5b The same serve kicks up and toward the returner's body on the forehand.

John Newcombe–Tony Roche

In the late '60s and the early '70s, Tony Roche and John Newcombe set the standard for men's doubles play. A team that had beaten them had beaten the best, and this was a real accomplishment. These two guys grew up together in Australia and then traveled the world as a tandem for about 25 years. They represented their country in Davis Cup play several times and, in fact, worked together in the '90s as a successful Davis Cup captain and coach. In their playing days, "Newk," a right-hander, was the captain on the court, exhibiting an air of great confidence and an intimidating manner. "Rochee," a left-hander, worked the team on the practice court with his no-nonsense style of play.

Newk and Rochee were very consistent as a team. There were no obvious weaknesses in their game, and they could hurt their opposition in many ways. Newcombe liked to take chances and make players pay for not getting the serve to his backhand. He would run around the second serve and belt the forehand at their feet, and when they looked up after hitting the shoestring volley he would be up at the net popping a volley right through them. He also liked to poach off his partner's return of serve, which was chipped off the backhand or topspinned off the forehand. Either way, opponents had to quickly move forward to hit the first volley off a short, low ball. If they didn't hit the volley firmly, Newk would poach, so there was a tendency for players to be looking at him instead of the ball.

As a serving team they had the advantage of presenting a different look on every service game. Newk had a heavy, deep first and second serve, which he followed quickly to the net. Rochee had a heavily sliced lefty delivery that stayed low, swinging away from a right-hander's backhand or into the body. It was hard to attack his serve even though it was not hit hard; by the time an opponent hit it, Tony was at the net. His backhand volley was considered a lethal weapon by the other pros. The goal was to try to return serve to his forehand volley, but he wasn't too weak on that side either. On top of that, John was always up at the net, ready to intercept any return that wasn't hit just right. So, it was very hard to break serve against this duo, and opponents had to work really hard to hold serve. Eventually they would break down their opponents and come up with another "W" (win).

Their style was aggressive, and their teamwork was effective. Because Newcombe and Roche were so consistent, they played well on both slow and fast surfaces. Their long-term partnership gave them the additional advantage of being able to anticipate each other's every possible move on the court.

As I mentioned earlier, returners don't know if the server will hit the first serve with great force or just roll the ball in. As in baseball, where the change-up can be quite effective if the batter is waiting for the fastball, this works to the server's advantage. I'll never forget playing against Arthur Ashe the first time. We played at the famous Los Angeles Tennis Club, on the center court. I had heard about his great booming first serve, so I had a game plan set to handle it: I would stand back behind the baseline about three or four feet. That would give me a little more time to react to the big bomb he would slam at me. I don't know if Arthur had read my mind (an 18-year-old, fairly unused mind), but he served his first serve at about two-thirds speed for the whole first set. My rhythm was totally off, and I kept popping the return of serve up for an easy, put-away volley. Also, because I was so far back, he kept hitting this slow, short, heavily sliced serve wide to my forehand that would take me into the side fence. I guess his four years of college tennis had taught him what worked in situations like this. I thought that at any moment he would hit the big one, so I stayed back until about midway through the second set. Having been physically bruised from running into the side fence and emotionally embarrassed for an hour, I finally moved up. You guessed it. He served a couple of bombs—end of match.

Imagine if you had three position variations, three spin variations, and three placement variations, and mixed those up with a couple speed variations. Who could ever get into a groove returning serve against you? All you have to do is practice serving from three positions, practice three different spin serves, practice hitting into the two corners as well as into the body, and work on doing all these things at different speeds (see chapter 7 for specific drills). It is as easy as that to give your favorite opponents enough variety to last a lifetime.

Net Player

I mentioned at the beginning of this chapter that in doubles you have the benefit of a partner who can help you win the games you serve. Winning is a team effort, and the server's partner can make a serve look better than it is or cause the team to lose more service games than it deserves to.

The net player can help complicate the job of the player returning serve. The net player must make the two opponents aware that he or she is there and is a force to be reckoned with. This is done through careful positioning and subtle movement. The net player can also direct what should happen on each point in the same way that a catcher does in baseball. Much of this direction is accomplished before the point by way of some simple communication between the two players. The communication can be done verbally or with signals. The verbal communication sometimes takes place on changeovers or between points.

Poaching

One of the points that is usually discussed and decided just before the serve is whether or not the net player is going to *poach,* that is, leave one side of the court to intercept a ball that has been directed to the other side of the court (see figure 4.6, *a* and *b*). The possibility of the net player poaching makes the game quite exciting, and it puts pressure on the player who is trying to return the serve.

Before I go into the various options associated with poaching, I want to mention that it is generally understood that a player will poach only on the first serve because he or she may be too vulnerable to try it on the second serve. I have seen teams that have poached on both serves equally, but normally if there is a poach that takes place on a second serve, it is after a pop-up return of serve or it is strictly a surprise gamble on the part of the net player. Both members of the serving team need to make certain that they are in accordance with whichever decision is made concerning poaching. You don't want to lose points unnecessarily because of a communication mix-up.

There are three ways to decide and communicate whether or not you will poach. One way, which is a little risky, is to decide on the changeover which points you are going to poach. For example, you may decide that you want

4.6a Crossing over to take a shot that would ordinarily be covered by your partner can upset the opposition. Here the net player moves to intercept a return.

to poach on the first and third points of the game. The advantage of this method is that your opponents have no prior warning of any kind that the poach is on. The challenge is that after a couple of points and during the heat of the battle you or your partner may forget about the decision made during the changeover. You may then experience one of those embarrassing moments when both members of your team are on one side of the court and no one is on the other. This method might work for you, but I don't recommend it because of the potential confusion.

The second way to direct the action is by using hand signals (see page 36). The net player generally gives these. You can use any predetermined signals you like as long as both players are absolutely certain what they mean. A simple system would be a closed fist to stay and an open hand to poach, or vice versa. I like using the open hand to stay (because it looks like "stop") and the closed fist to go. More advanced teams may give the signal to go or stay as well as a signal as to where to serve.

The other common method of communicating whether or not you will poach is by speaking to one another briefly before each point. This requires constant meetings, but it does make it just about impossible to miscommunicate or have your plan stolen. During your visit you can decide what to do for both serves, including how to handle the second serve should

4.6b This shot will hit its mark. The net player sends the ball right to the feet of the opposing net player.

you miss the first. I like this method of communicating for two reasons. First, it gets both players involved on every point, so neither of you will be tempted to mentally float or tune out for even a short time. Second, it keeps your opponents wondering what you might do and second-guessing the strategy. I think there is a tendency for teams to overthink the game, and therefore to play worse, when they see their opponents whispering sweet nothings to each other.

Here's an example of how this kind of communication can make the other team uncomfortable. If the net player goes back to say something to the server on the first point and proceeds to poach, then the next time they get together the returning team will assume that the poach is on. If the net player does not poach on the second point, by the time the server and net player conference before the third point, the receiving team will have no idea what to expect. There is then a tendency for the returning team to look at the net player (and not at the ball) to see what he or she is going to do. It is hard enough to hit the ball while watching it with two eyes, let alone while watching the net player with one eye and the ball with the other.

Poaching is not always successful. In fact, the first few times you try it, you will probably have some problems. The most important thing to remember is that if you commit to your partner, who is serving, that you are going to poach, then you must poach! I have seen players say they are going to poach, start to do so, and then stop, saying that they couldn't reach the cross-court return. The player who is poaching must realize that when he or she moves across, his or her partner is moving quickly to the side that the poacher is evacuating. If the poaching player stops, then *no one* will be able to get to that cross-court return. As with a marriage, when you make a commitment you must honor it. Your partner is counting on you.

One quick piece of advice applies if people are watching your doubles match. If you say that you are going to poach and then immediately realize that you can't get to the ball, you can say "yours" so that the people in the stands will think the loss of the point was your partner's fault. You just might fool that audience. (Of course, you should keep in mind that you might also lose a partner if you pull this too many times!)

The most important aspect of poaching is timing. Experiment with your timing while playing points. You want to be able to cover almost any cross-court return. That means that you must make your move soon enough that you can reach the return, but not so soon that you telegraph your intention or open up your side of the court too early. The timing of the move depends on several factors.

The first factor is how hard your partner serves the ball. If he or she serves it very hard then you must move soon so that, if the ball comes back, you will be able to get to it. If your partner serves a big serve with a lot of spin or a change-up and you move early, your opponent will see what you're doing and will hit behind you. If the returner is standing way back, leave later. If the returner is inside the baseline or usually hits a hard return, leave early. If he or she just chips the ball back, you can leave later.

Maybe the most important element is how fast you are. If you have a quick first step and can accelerate fast, then you can wait until your opponent makes contact with the return. If you are very slow, you may want to start *before* your partner serves (just kidding—no one is that slow). It really helps to practice poaching with the same partner so that you get used to his or her serving style. You don't have to be a Speedy Gonzales to be an effective poacher. There is nothing more fun in doubles than turning an opponent's good return into a put-away volley right through the opposing team's net player.

Optimal Positioning

The net player does not always have to start in the traditional position. I have seen many different variations in starting positions leave the opposition wondering what to do or at least asking themselves, "Why?" Sometimes when a team is asking the "why" question, the opposing team starts winning. My philosophy is not to change a winning game, but to try to change a losing game. In the higher levels of competition, however, it is sometimes necessary to make some subtle changes while the team is still winning to prevent the opponents from catching on and beginning to get into a groove. John Newcombe once said that when he played Rod Laver in singles or doubles, he would always be looking ahead even when he was in the lead, so that Laver would not get the chance to catch on to his strategy.

Generally, the net player should stand at the net and in the other half of the court (see figure 4.7). The most bizarre formation I have ever seen was at the Orange Bowl, in one of the larger International junior events. The net player stood *to the left of the server on the baseline* when his partner was serving to the ad court. He didn't like to volley, but he did like to hit huge forehands from the baseline. These guys were good international juniors, but in a match against good professional doubles players, this formation would guarantee them a second place finish.

One relatively common formation is the Australian formation, so called because the Aussies were the first to use it (see figure 4.8). In this formation the net player stands on the same side of the court in front of the server, and the server comes toward the net on a diagonal, instead of a straightforward path after serving. This formation is quite effective against teams that can hit returns of serve well cross court but don't like to hit down the line. If you are playing a team for the first time and one player is killing you with a great cross-court return, then try this formation occasionally or until your opponent hurts you with the down-the-line return. If he or she hurts you with that return as well, then you are in big trouble anyway. Sometimes this formation can turn a match around very quickly and thereby frustrate your opponents.

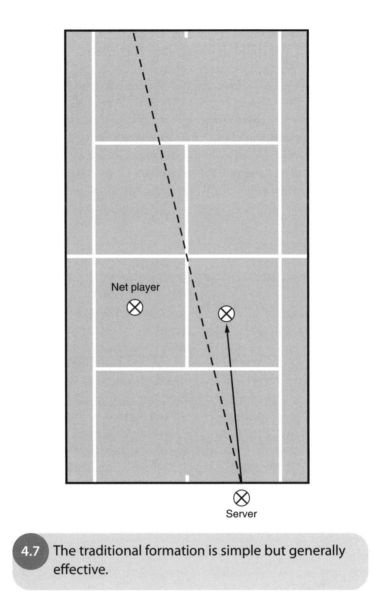

4.7 The traditional formation is simple but generally effective.

Some teams use this formation on key points, such as breakpoint. Again, using this formation makes your opponents think—and they just might think too much or think their way past hitting a smart shot.

Similar to the Australian formation is the I-formation. Here the net player stands right in the middle of the court, straddling the center service line. This means that the player will have to duck down or risk getting hit with the

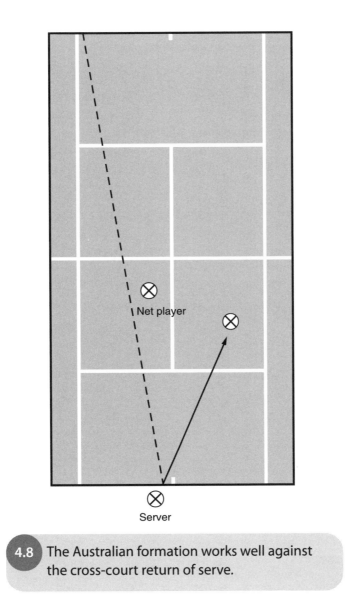

Net player

Server

4.8 The Australian formation works well against the cross-court return of serve.

serve as it whizzes over his or her head (see figure 4.9). This formation really keeps the opponents guessing because when the serve is hit, the net player goes to one side or the other, and the server covers the side that the net player does not cover. So every time the serve is put into play the returner has to decide which way to hit the ball, either cross court or down the line. The execution of this strategy must be very precise and feature

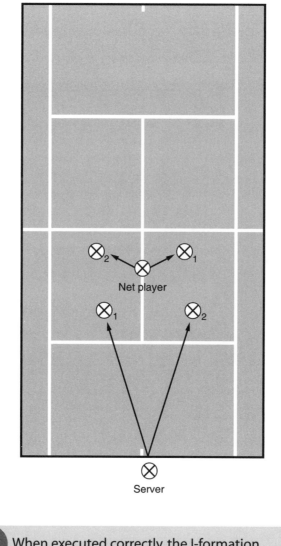

Net player

Server

4.9 When executed correctly, the I-formation creates uncertainty and confusion for the returning team.

perfect communication and timing. The players must also move quickly for it to be effective. As with any other variation, if you don't need to try this, don't, but if you are losing by playing the traditional formation, mixing up the formations for a few games just might turn the match around. If you sense that your opponents are getting into a groove with their returns, it may be time to vary your formation; by changing the formation you make your opponents think about why you are doing so, and that in and of itself can negatively affect their performance. If you do use this formation, be sure to practice it before trying it in an important match. When it is done well the I-formation is fun to watch, and some returning teams become very confused and frustrated when they are up against it.

In all of these basic positions or variations, the net player needs to be active at the net. This means that he or she should move occasionally from the starting position to poach but also be alert for any chance to take advantage of a weak return. The idea is not to let your foes get away with anything but a quality shot. One thing that the net player can do, no matter what starting position he or she uses, is fake a move so that the returner will see the movement out of the corner of his or her eye and be distracted while attempting the return of serve. Now some players get carried away and jump all over the place. I think that such behavior is bush league and represents bad sportsmanship. Keep your opponents off balance by playing well, varying your positioning, using smart strategy, and moving at the right time.

Good mixed doubles teams try a lot of poaching and position variations. In a mixed doubles match, a quick male player will want to try some different poaching and position variations to put pressure on the returning team. If the female player is good at the net and her partner has a good serve, then she can take advantage by knocking off some weak returns. Many teams feel the need to gamble a bit to try to hold serve on the female player's serve, and this calls for movement at the net. Finding the right balance, taking some chances but not too many chances, is always tricky. Experiment a little as you play, and you will discover when and how your team can use poaching and formation changes to make the most of your service game.

Defusing the Serve
With a Potent Return

The return of serve is the second most important shot in the game of doubles. If you have a good return of serve you can defuse that big weapon—the serve. When you see good doubles players in action, you'll notice that they put a lot of balls back in play, forcing the servers to hit more volleys than perhaps they would like.

The key concept to remember when returning the serve is that you are not supposed to *win* the games in which your opponents are serving. Therefore you should approach these games with something of a gambling attitude and take some chances to make things happen. One of the reasons I like to serve first in a doubles match is the fun of being able to gamble when our team is returning serve. I usually choose to serve first in singles as well, but I might occasionally serve second under certain circumstances, such as when my serve is really feeling bad or when I know that my opponents have a weak serve or tend to start slowly. If you can hold your serve, then your opponents will be under pressure just to stay even. When it gets to 4–5 and 5–6, you can really shake up your opponents by trying something new or just going for your shots. If you happen to lose your serve at 4–all or 5–all, then you still have a chance to break back and avoid losing the set.

If you are having problems with the return of serve, then you may be guilty of ignoring the five most basic objectives of this part of the game. Work to meet the following goals, in the order in which they are listed:

1. Get your racket on the serve. This most fundamental goal applies mainly to the first serves your opponent fires at you. If you are getting aced a lot or are barely touching the serve, then be patient and wait for that inevitable game in which your opponent misses a few first serves. In doubles you rarely see a lot of aces because of the increased importance of the server's getting a high percentage of first serves in the court. Servers generally take a little pace off the first serve to avoid giving their opponents the opportunity to exploit the easier second serve that follows a miss.

You may wonder why getting a high percentage of first serves in is an even more important concept in doubles. As I mentioned in chapter 4, the doubles server is trying to stay on the offensive and does not want to give opponents too many easy second serves to attack. In addition, most good doubles teams come in behind their serves, and it is difficult for servers to volley when their adversaries are hitting aggressive returns at their feet as they rush to the net. In singles a player can stay back and not be hurt much by having to hit a lot of second serves, but in doubles having to stay back is a big penalty for good players. Later in this chapter I'll explain what you can do if you are not even getting your racket on the serve.

2. Get the ball back over the net and into the court. The second goal also relates primarily to returning first serves. Many teams play ineffective doubles simply because they don't keep the ball in play on the return of serve. These teams try to do too much against servers who are hitting the ball well. The ambitious tactic of trying to hit the ball through the combatants, as opposed to simply making them play a low shot, does not normally pay off in the long run.

It is important to remember that it's possible for your opponents to miss groundstrokes when they stay back and to miss volleys and overheads when they are at the net. They can even miss easy shots—real sitters. Many times my partner or I have just barely managed to get a racket on the ball and have floated a shot back that we thought couldn't be missed, only to see—to our surprise as well that of our opponents—a careless or nervous mistake by the other team. Often, these mistakes occur during critical points and can turn a losing match around.

Recently, I was playing in a no-ad situation; it was game point for both teams in a round-robin contest, so whoever won the game won our division. Our opponents hit a big, wide serve that my partner just barely returned over the net. The opposing net player had an easy volley in the middle of the court, but he dumped it into the net. The four of us couldn't believe it. The simple concept of getting the ball back and giving the other team a chance to hit the ball again is more important than you might think. You never know when your opponents might miss.

3. Get the ball back to the server's feet. If the server serves and volleys, then your objective is to hit the ball short, inside the service line, so that the server will have to hit a low volley or half-volley. Because the server will have to hit up without a great deal of pace, this should create an opportunity for you to hit an offensive shot next. If the server normally stays back after serving, then you should hit the return deep so that the server will have to hit the next shot from behind the baseline. If, in the heat of battle, you forget these last few lines of advice, just remember that you are trying to return the serve toward your opponents' *feet* no matter where they are in the court. If you do that, you won't go wrong unless your opponents serve and run back toward the back fence. If that is the case, you probably have them so intimidated that you don't need any of my advice.

4. Take the net. The ultimate goal is to hit the return and come in behind it, in an attempt to take the net away from your foes. You can do this with an aggressive driving return or with a chip and charge approach that allows you to control the return and take some pace off the ball as you dip it at their feet. Whichever approach you choose, this maneuver will be daunting for your opponents, whether they serve and volley or serve and stay back, because if you succeed you will be in charge and they will be on the defensive. This is usually easier to accomplish off the second serve, so an attempt to use this technique may encourage your opponents to make the most of the first serves. Even if you sometimes miss the return, it really is intimidating for the server to look down at a low volley and then look up to see you flying in for the kill. As with any means of keeping your opponents off balance, using this tactic may mean that you lose a couple of battles but it should help you win the war.

5. Vary your return. It is of great benefit to prevent your opponents from being certain of the direction the ball will come from. Be proactive and plant the seed in their minds that, especially on second serves, you are not always going to do the same thing. This uncertainty will keep the serving team from poaching and moving as much as they might like. I'll describe some varieties of return shots later in this chapter.

Billie Jean King–Rosie Casals

In the late 1960s and early 1970s, Billie Jean King was the Queen of the women's game. With her partner, Rosie Casals, Billie was also dominant on the doubles court. In the King–Casals era, three of the four grand slam events were played on grass: the Australian Open, Wimbledon, and the US Open. When Billie Jean and Rosie played on the grass courts, they were able to serve and volley well because they were quick and athletic. They were not very tall, but they were two balls of energy on the court.

Besides being a dominant force on the singles and doubles court, Billie Jean King did more for the women's game and for the women's movement than any other sportswoman of her time. Her confrontation with Bobby Riggs in the "Battle of the Sexes" in 1972 provided exposure to women's tennis and to the game in general. Her ability to handle the pressure and beat Bobby gave her confidence that carried over into her doubles game. Like all the great singles and doubles champions, she thrived on the big moments of the game.

Rosie was particularly quick and effective at the net, even though she was only about 5' 2". She loved to "mix it up" in those quick volley exchanges that take place when all four players are eye-to-eye at the net. Her serve was not overpowering, but she would get to the net quickly and volley soundly. When she and Billie Jean played together, they would take chances by poaching a lot and keeping their opponents guessing. This strategy would eventually wear down their foes and cause the other team to make some errors.

Both women were right-handers, and Rosie would play the deuce court while Billie took the ad. Billie did not have the left-handed forehand that so many of the great teams had on the ad side, but she did have a great backhand that was quite effective on break points. She liked to go for it when she had the opportunity, and this made her dangerous, especially when her opponents missed the first serve.

The strong spirit shared by Billie Jean King and Rosie Casals on the court put fear into the hearts of their opponents and set them apart from their colleagues.

Just as the serving team works together, members of the returning team, the returner and the returning net player, should work as a unit and help each other to break serve. An active returning net player can really make the returner look good. The returning net player plays an important role in keeping the serving team off balance, especially when they are hitting their first volley.

Mary Lou Piatek, shown here with partner Virginia Wade, demonstrates a potent return. Piatek meets the ball with the center of the racket and is in good balance at the point of contact.

The strength and type of return of serve is an important part of determining each partner's positions, when to poach, and how to play out the points. As the returner and his or her partner get comfortable and experiment with different returns of serve and different strategies to use after the return, they can better determine how to take advantage of each partner's strengths and weaknesses. Start by analyzing how quick each player is at the net and how comfortable each player is crossing the court. Generally it is easier to poach on the forehand side because the player has better reach; that factor can be a determiner of which side a player should chose (all other things being equal).

Some players move to the backhand volley better and therefore are more effective playing the deuce side and poaching on ad points. Roy Emerson, who won 16 Grand Slam doubles tournaments, was the best I have ever seen playing the deuce side. When his partner hit a good return, he frequently would cross and, even on low balls, nail the backhand volley and keep it in.

 Returner

The return of serve must be executed as quickly as a baseball batter's swing. When the fastball comes at him at 95 miles an hour, the batter's reaction time must be within hundredths of a second. The first serve by a player at the women's and men's pro level may come at the returner as fast as 120 to140 miles per hour, and even though the bounce slows it down quite a bit, there is precious little time to react. I hope that you are not playing someone who can serve that fast, but whether you are or aren't, the same fundamentals apply. Adhering to the fundamental concepts will give you the best chance to successfully return any serve.

Remember to focus on the ball as the server releases the toss. Start by bending your knees and bending slightly at the waist before the serve. As the toss is released, slowly rise into a good ready position and split step as the ball is struck. This initiates the movement to the ball. Next comes a quick shoulder turn as the racket starts its way back. Sometimes, with a very fast delivery, this shoulder turn and a short back-and-forward swing at the ball is all that you'll have time to do. With a slower serve, you can take of couple of steps to the ball and transfer your weight into the shot with a forward step toward the target. Try practicing this quick shoulder turn, on or off the court, while simulating the return of serve.

Positioning

The first thing a returner needs to think about is not how hard he or she can hit the return, but how to get the ball back over the net in a consistent manner. As I mentioned in chapter 3, it's important to start in a position that affords the best chance to return the first serve no matter where it is hit.

In figure 5.1, *a* through *d*, you can see that the positioning of the returner depends on the server's position and the type of serve he or she is prone to produce. Every server has a favorite serve, just as every pitcher has a favorite pitch. If you are playing someone who is just trying to get the ball in, then your job as a returner is going to be easy. The better the competition, the more likely you are to face players who can hit at least the first serve with some pace, variety, and accuracy.

After playing a team a few times, you'll get a feel for what type of serve your opponents are likely to hit and where you need to be positioned to return that serve most consistently and effectively. Try to pick up the server's patterns and tendencies so that you can anticipate what type of serve and placement he or she will attempt on big points. I have played against some teams that would *always* hit a kick first serve to my backhand on a break point, knowing that if they missed the first serve, I would try to run around my backhand on the second serve and hit a big forehand return. This was great for my partner and me; armed with that almost certain knowledge, I

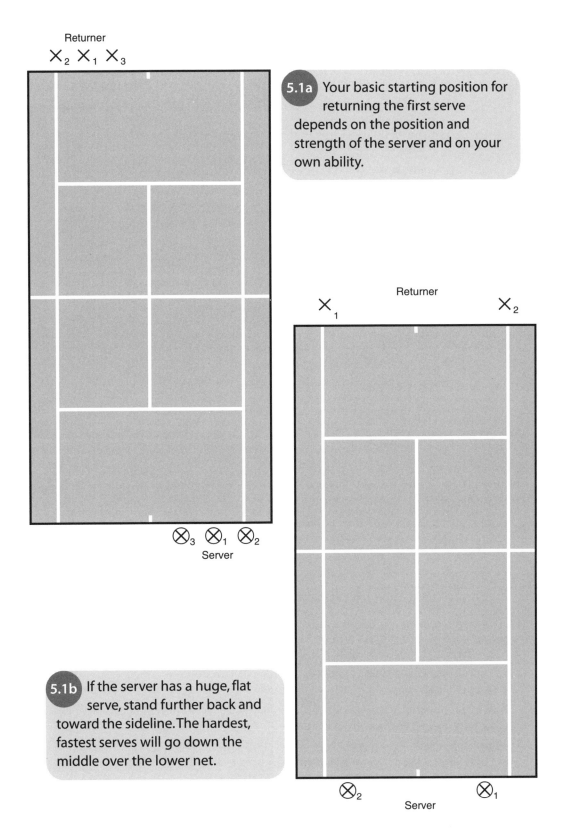

Returner
X₂ X₁ X₃

5.1a Your basic starting position for returning the first serve depends on the position and strength of the server and on your own ability.

Returner

X₁   X₂

⊗₃ ⊗₁ ⊗₂
Server

5.1b If the server has a huge, flat serve, stand further back and toward the sideline. The hardest, fastest serves will go down the middle over the lower net.

⊗₂   ⊗₁
Server

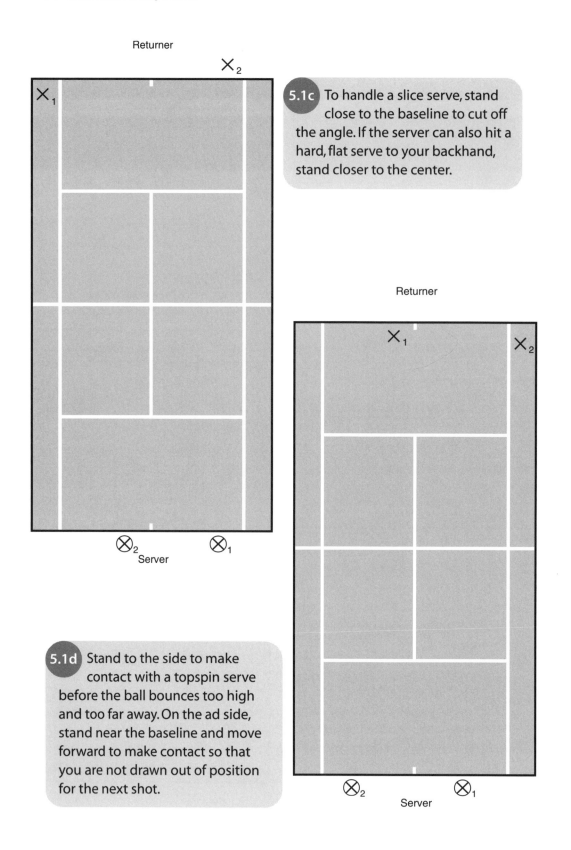

Returner

X₂

X₁

⊗₂ ⊗₁
Server

5.1c To handle a slice serve, stand close to the baseline to cut off the angle. If the server can also hit a hard, flat serve to your backhand, stand closer to the center.

Returner

X₁ X₂

⊗₂ ⊗₁
Server

5.1d Stand to the side to make contact with a topspin serve before the ball bounces too high and too far away. On the ad side, stand near the baseline and move forward to make contact so that you are not drawn out of position for the next shot.

could be physically and mentally prepared to hit the return, and my partner would know that the return would be coming from the backhand swing. But you can't always count on the ball coming to a particular spot.

Types of Returns

There are four types of returns you can hit with consistent success: the block, the drive, the chip and charge, and the lob. Each type of return is appropriate against different serves and styles of play. Some of the great players only hit the ball one way, but they do it so well that they are very effective against anyone. But most good players can hit at least a couple of these types of returns and can adjust to different serves as needed.

Block

The block return uses the server's pace, so it can be hit pretty hard, but its hallmark is that it is hit with control. The way to get that control is to take a short backswing and use a very compact followthrough (see figure 5.2, *a* through *d*). The block is usually hit with a little bit of underspin to take some pace off the oncoming serve and to help direct the ball right to the server's shoestrings.

The returner may play back behind the baseline to gain more time to react to the first serve and to have a better chance to get a racket on the ball for the block. He or she may also stand in close and take the serve early to give the server less time to get close to the net. This latter style is preferable because it rushes the server and puts pressure on him or her to run a little faster and react a little quicker to try to handle a tough shot. This style is also more difficult, especially against a hard serve, but with practice you'll find that it is not as hard as it looks.

The block return requires good timing and the ability to consistently pick up the ball early. As with all first serves, a quick shoulder turn after the split step initiates the backswing. Against big serves, that is all the preparation that is needed to hit the ball. The backswing should continue a bit after the shoulder turn. The shot will be similar to a volley, with variations on the amount of spin. When I was "on," I would hit the block return fairly flat. If I was struggling for control, I would hit it with more underspin.

Generally, the returner is not thinking of coming to the net behind the return but is looking to do something offensive with the second shot, if possible. This might include such tactics as hitting through the middle, hitting hard at the right hip of an opponent, going down the line, or possibly throwing up an offensive lob over the opponents if they are closing in too much. You can think of this tactic as a one-two punch, with the emphasis on the *two*. Getting the return back down at the server's feet is the goal on the first shot, and doing more damage is the goal on the second (or possibly the third or fourth) shot.

5.2a A split step just as the serve is hit sets up the block return.

5.2b A short backswing maximizes control.

The advantage of the block return is the short, compact stroke, which uses the opponent's serving speed to get the ball back over the net with control and accuracy. The disadvantage is that it is not as powerful and aggressive as some other returns.

Using the block return also gives a returner the option of switching and hitting a lob return of serve because the preparation is similar for the two shots. When the racket is back, the returner can just open up the racket face to elevate the ball over the net player's head. Knowing that he or she can't start too close to the net without being vulnerable to a possible lob will keep the net player on the alert.

The block return of serve was a popular choice for players of my era. It was, and still is, very effective against most teams because it forces servers to hit many tough, low volleys and to continue to play the rest of the point.

Woodbridge and Woodforde were exceptionally good at using the block return; they got a very high percentage of returns into play even against the best servers, then they moved toward the center of the court (taking

5.2c Hitting the block return with underspin reduces the pace and adjusts the direction.

5.2d A strong, compact followthrough toward the target completes this powerful, controlled shot.

advantage of their left-handed/right-handed combination) and hit a forehand on the next shot. Their returns wouldn't blow the opposition away, but eventually their consistency would take a toll. After a while the other team would try too hard to win the point early so that they wouldn't have to deal with the next shot. In the 1999 Davis Cup final in Nice against France, the "Woodies" started off playing very poorly; to everyone's surprise, they were not getting many returns of serve in court even though the match was on red clay. After struggling for nearly two sets, they finally *came good* (as the Aussies would say), and from that point forward they missed only a handful of returns of serve. In response, the Frenchmen started trying to go for more on their serves and also tried to hit their first volleys harder and closer to the lines. This was not a typical start for the Woodies, but it was a normal ending for them in that they ultimately suffocated the French with their solid offensive play.

Drive

This style of return is increasingly popular in doubles play in college and on the pro tour. Because of the bigger, stronger, lighter rackets, the players are hitting the ball harder; the young players are going for the return of serve more instead of just keeping the ball in play. The really good players who return well in singles are getting a fairly high percentage of drive returns into the court, but many others swing wildly and are unable to get most returns of serve back into play. In doubles the target is smaller (half the court), and good volleyers can handle hard returns coming right to them by blocking the volley back. This results in some spectacular shots and some very difficult volleys, but they are accomplished less by finesse and more by *working* the points.

The drive can be hit flat, but generally it is hit with topspin to allow more control and to bring the ball back down into the court after it travels over the net. It is difficult to be consistent with the drive because the swing is usually pretty big, with a quick shoulder turn. When the first serve is hit into the corner, forcing the returner to stretch, the player's timing and connection

5.3a The drive return begins with a split step as the serve is hit.

5.3b A quick shoulder turn and a long backswing produce great acceleration and power.

with the contact point must be very precise to put the ball into the court (see figure 5.3, *a* through *d*). I generally recommend that a player who wants to be aggressive on all returns of serve at least try to take a shorter backswing when the first serve is being delivered. Then, on the second serve return, which comes in slower, he or she will have more time to take a bigger swing at the ball.

The shot preparation for the drive is very similar to that for the block return, with a good split step at the time of the server's contact with the ball and then a quick shoulder turn to initiate the backswing. With the drive, the backswing will go further back than it does in the block, so there will be more acceleration of the swing and more power in the return. The backswing will be lower if topspin is desired, so that the followthrough will naturally finish above the shoulder (see figure 5.3*d*). This shot will get back to the server quickly and, if it goes in, will require good hands to control the volley on the move. The uncertain odds that this aggressive drive return is going to go in makes it an unreliable type of return to attempt.

In mixed doubles, if the female server doesn't serve as hard as the male server, both players on the returning team may try to drive the female

5.3c Good contact on a drive return with topspin sends the ball upward and forward.

5.3d A high followthrough finishes the drive return with topspin.

server's first serve back and to block the male server's first serve. The female returner may stand further back and lob the male server's first serve high and deep just to make the other team hit another ball or to take advantage of the opposing female player's lack of a good overhead or inability to move back quickly. During the second serve, both the male and female returners may try to drive the serve back. The returners might prefer to chip and charge against the female server, if she stays back on her serve.

Chip and Charge

The chip-and-charge return of serve is very effective, but it is not used as often today on the pro tour as it once was. The serves of today are harder, and players who are trying to be more aggressive with their returns of serve tend to use drives. Still, when players execute the chip and charge well, they can take apart a team that is not used to it.

The idea with the chip and charge is that the returner moves into the return, hits it with underspin to take some pace off the shot for more control, and then tries to beat the server to the net. If this return is hit properly and the ball is dumped at the incoming server's feet, the server is under tremendous pressure to hit a volley that the returner can't hit back down at him or her. Since players are used to hitting the ball aggressively and staying back in

5.4a The split step sets up the chip and charge return.

5.4b The chip and charge return should be "punched" in front of the body. It should be directed forward and slightly downward.

singles tennis, they are often unprepared to handle the doubles chip and charge. With a little bit of practice hitting the ball off the rise and moving forward, you can get very good at this technique. If your opponents stay back on their serve, then you have taken the net away from them and placed your team in command.

Like the block return, the chip and charge shot is somewhat similar to a volley; it requires a quick shoulder turn after the split step (see figure 5.4*a*) but also requires forward movement through the shot. Take a short backswing, and hit the ball in front of your body with more of a punch than a full swing as you move toward the net (see figure 5.4, *b* and *c*). Use an underspin hit to direct the ball slightly downward as well as forward; this keeps the ball from flying up on you. The forehand and two-handed backhand shot can be blocked with a short swing to control the ball that will still allow you to move into the court behind the return. Many two-handed backhand players don't underspin the ball, but because they use two hands on the racket they can control the ball better than a player hitting a one-handed backhand.

As they move toward the net, players will feel like they are almost carrying the ball forward. Usually, the ball is not hit with a great deal of pace. The chip-and-charge return is very effective against players who don't like low volleys. One disadvantage is that if it is not hit well, opponents can poach and knock off the return before it gets to the incoming server. On the other hand, you can more easily shift to a lob from the chip and charge than from a drive. This can be helpful against a team that is poaching quite a bit.

5.4c A moderate followthrough and continued movement toward the net complete the chip-and-charge return.

The Lob

In general, there are two types of lobs—the offensive and defensive lobs. The offensive lob can be hit with excessive topspin, flat, or with underspin. Today the most common shot hit by the pros is the lob with excessive topspin. This shot is used in a passing shot situation with one or both opponents at the net. Players who have heavy topspin groundstrokes are able to disguise this shot well because the backswing is very similar. The flat lob is effective when the opponents close in on the net and are guessing as to which way the passing shot is going to be hit. The chip and underspin offensive lob works well if the opponents are closing in to cut off the delicate chip and the returner fools them by going up over their heads as they are leaning forward (see figure 5.5, *a* through *d*).

The defensive lob is hit when a player is out of court, usually behind the baseline. The chances of hitting a winning passing shot in this situation are low if the opponents are in good position at the net and the returner is not in control of the point. This shot is used primarily to make the opponents hit another shot but also to keep them from playing too close to the net.

The lob is an interesting and effective shot because many players find it difficult to move back quickly enough to hit the overhead. They may also lack confidence in their ability to hit the overhead, especially if it is windy or the sun is in their eyes. Often the first reaction by players on a doubles team to a lob hit by the opposition is to yell out "yours." On the other hand, the majority of pros like seeing a lob go up because they assume that they will be able to win the point. I believe that a good lob return of serve (or lob during the point), even at the highest level of play, can be very effective and can help a team win a good number of points.

Since the serves are generally hit hard, the return of serve lob is seldom hit aggressively. With male and female players at the pro level returning serve more aggressively, hitting a surprise lob return of serve is not as easy or effective as a block return. Once you take the racket back to hit a drive or topspin return, you commit to that type of shot, and it is hard to change. Returners who hit the chip and charge, with its higher and more compact backswing, can pretty easily hit a disguised lob.

Woodbridge and Woodforde used the lob effectively throughout their partnership. Their return of serve style was perfect for this tactic. Both of them would hit the backhand block return of serve quite a bit, and they would look for the opportunity to hit the lob at key points during the match. If they noticed that their opponents were close to the net or poaching quite a bit, they wouldn't hit the lob right away or hit it all the time. They would file away this information away in their internal computers (their heads) and wait for a breakpoint or tight situation. Then one of them would hit the shot. Because they practiced this shot incessantly, they would almost lick their chops anticipating the perfect moment to spring it on their opponents. It was beautiful to watch. The opponents would keep moving closer and

5.5a It's helpful to take the ball early to begin the lob return.

5.5b A high followthrough is required for the overhead lob.

5.5c It's difficult for the net player to move backward while tracking the lob.

5.5d A player may need to use a big, scissors-kick jump to reach a well-placed lob.

closer to the net, with an eye toward pouncing on the cross-court return of serve. Then all of a sudden they would desperately struggle to get back or call to their partner to try to cover the well-disguised deep lob. Once the ball appeared to be clearing their opponents' heads and they could see that both players were on the retreat, the Woodies would quickly move forward to take over at the net.

The backswing for the lob return of serve must be short, with the racket open (racket facing slightly upward). Use a long followthrough to ensure good length on the shot. The return should be aimed over the backhand side of the net player and executed in such a way that it will favor the middle of the court if it does not go exactly where it is aimed (see figure 5.5*e*).

The offensive lob, which would most likely be hit after the serving team hits their first volley, is hit in a manner similar to that used to hit a groundstroke. This is why it is so deceptive. If a team is hitting good groundstrokes, the volleying team usually plays fairly close to the net so that the ball doesn't dip down at their feet. But it's hard for a team to simultaneously cover the dipping groundstroke and the topspin lob if the opponents hit them both well. Great back-court players may be at a disadvantage when they play at the net, but they can make up for it with good dipping shots and topspin lobs.

The topspin lob is hit with an exaggerated low-to-high swing and excessive topspin, both of which cause the ball to come down quickly after clearing the net player's head. This shot bounces away from the net, so once it goes over a player's head it is almost impossible to run down.

5.5e If the lob return misses, it should go toward the center of the court.

Returning the Second Serve

Most people prefer one style of return, but it is best to be able to hit many types of returns so that you can adjust to the different styles of players that you come up against. No matter what your favorite style of return you can be more aggressive when you return the second serve. As I explained in chapter 3, the mindset for returning the second serve is very different. Your opponents have given you an opening; you'll want to hit your strongest shot and take full advantage of a second serve opportunity. Let's assume that you have a stronger forehand than backhand and that you are waiting for the second delivery. Stand over to the left and move inside the baseline (see figure 5.6); from there you have four options.

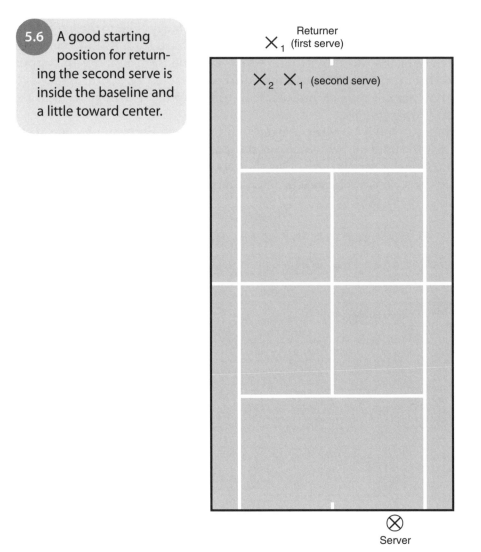

5.6 A good starting position for returning the second serve is inside the baseline and a little toward center.

1. You can stay forward and to the left.
2. You can start forward and left, then as the opponent tosses the ball, move back to a neutral position, forward and middle.
3. You can start in a neutral position and then move to the left as the opponent tosses the ball.
4. You can start in the neutral position and stay there.

By applying these different positions in second serve situations, the first thing you do is make your opponents wonder what you are trying to do. Second, by encouraging your opponents to guess what you will do, you may cause them to break their concentration on their primary responsibility: serving. Third, they may guess wrong and give you the shot you want, or they may guess correctly but still put the ball where you can hit it. They may try to serve wide (to the right), thinking that you are moving left, or try to serve into the small areas in order to force you to hit your weaker shot, the backhand. If they serve to the right and you are there (in scenarios #2 and #4 above), then you have the shot you wanted. If they serve to the right but serve slower because it is a second serve, you will probably still get your racket on the ball. If they try to serve close to the line on your backhand side and miss, it's your point.

I have found that early in a match a server may be able to use the opening you created to hurt you with the second serve. But when it is 15–40 or 30–40, the server is going to be a little tighter and more tentative, and bad things are more likely to happen for him or her. The server may take a gamble that works, hit the ball right where you want it, or double-fault.

If you do get the strong shot you wanted and you hit it hard, then you will have planted a seed in your opponents' mind. They will not want to see that hard hit come at them again. To prevent that, the server may start hitting an easier first serve to ensure that it goes in and to avoid having to hit a second serve. This puts you in a more favorable position; you are more likely to get easier first serves and to be able to place your returns where you want them.

It is also easier to drive, to block, and especially to chip and charge on second serves. When Bob Lutz chipped and charged on the second serve and put the ball low at our opponent's feet, while I was at the net and he was charging forward, we usually won the point.

Another good variation for returning the second serve is to hit right at the net player or down his or her alley. You should tell your partner you are going to attempt this shot. If your partner is ready and you hit the return of serve well, one of three things could happen. Your partner will get to put away a mis-hit reflex shot from the net player, you will have an easy second shot, or, ideally, you will win the point outright. This shot keeps the net player thinking about protecting the alley instead of doing a lot of poaching. Another added benefit, if the net player gets hit or passed or embarrassed, is that he or she may strongly encourage the server to get that first serve in the court.

In mixed doubles, the male player should try to use these variations to intimidate his opponent's second serve. It is good strategy to hit the male player's second serve at the female player at the net, or, if the female player's second serve is weak, to rip it at the male player at the net. When the female player is serving, return the serve with controlled aggression.

Returner's Partner

The success of the team that is returning serve depends on exactly that—the team. Certainly the player who is returning the serve is the key, but his or her partner is also very important in determining the success or failure of the team. The partner influences the opponents' ability to handle a good return and can save the point if the returner hits a less than desirable shot. I always said that I gave Bob Lutz all sorts of opportunities to make spectacular saves, reflexing shots for winners, on balls that he was able to touch only because of my high-floating, ineffective returns. I made him famous, but I was also responsible for a few black and blue spots on those occasions when, instead of Bob hitting the ball, the ball hit him.

As I mentioned in chapter 3, everything is dictated by the return. After making a call for the returner, the partner should look right at the serving team's net player to determine where the return has been directed. From that point on, the player can poach and assert his or her will on the opponents, just as the server's partner does on the other side of the net.

When a block return is hit, the returning team's net player is looking for a low return at the opponent's feet that will force him or her to hit the ball up. If it is a great low return, then the volleyer will not be able to hit the ball very hard; this will give the returning net player time to intercept the volley.

You might as well gamble and poach when your partner hits a good return of serve; you are not expecting to win the game that your opponents are serving so it doesn't hurt too much if you are not successful. And if you do move enough to plant that seed of uncertainty in your opponent's mind, you may reap dividends when the match becomes really tight. You might get an easy volley or force your opponents into making a mistake while they are trying to guess what you are going to do. Because the block return takes some of the pace off the ball, the returner's partner needs to wait an instant longer before moving to intercept the volley. The returner's partner must be able to act reflexively to cover all sorts of shots. If the returner is hitting pretty hard, the partner's starting position should be closer to the center line in order to put a little pressure on the volleyer. If the returner is not having an easy time, the partner should play a little more toward the alley. The returner's partner should split step as the volley is being hit, so that he or she can cut in any direction to hit a volley or even an overhead.

On the chip-and-charge return, the returner's partner will not poach as much because the returner is coming in behind the return. The returner's partner may move forward slightly to increase the pressure on the volleyer; the volley has to be very precise to keep it away from the two people at the net. If the return is hit well and the net player doesn't poach, then the returning team is in great shape to win the point. Don't hinder your team's opportunity to capitalize on the chip and charge by poaching and leaving the alley open.

On the drive return, the ball will be hit by the incoming server very quickly, so the partner must be ready to get into the act very soon. The only way the team can take advantage of the drive is for the partner to be alert and sensitive to the speed of the shot. When the drive return is hit well, the volleyer can get caught and be forced to struggle with an awkward volley or a tough groundstroke if he or she serves and stays back. The net player needs to keep his or her feet moving and keep the racket out in front. From this ready position, the net player will be ready to handle most of the shots that come his or her way. Given the speed of the shots, the returner's partner will probably not move too far. On drive returns, this player's job consists of reacting, reflexing, and defending.

The lob return is tricky for the returner's partner. If the lob is not high enough, the partner's life may be in jeopardy. If the lob goes over the opposing players' heads and the returner comes in to the net, then the opposition is likely to assume a defensive position and hit a lob for their next shot. Servers must let their partner know if they are even thinking about hitting a lob return of serve, so that the partner can be ready for a booming overhead or a sitter volley.

The returner's partner can adjust his or her position according to the quality of the return. This change in position can have a very big effect on the opponents. They will wonder why, and this alone will cause them to play a little differently. The main change a returner's partner can make is to stay back by the baseline with the returner. This takes away the opponents' target, if the return is hit poorly. Some players like to have a target because it causes them to hit more decisively. Without a target, the volleyer may not do as much with the shot, thereby giving the returning team another decent swing at the next ball. *When* you change your return formation is key. If you have consistently been struggling to break serve during the first set, make the change at 5–4 or 6–5. The other team will have been rolling along and will all of a sudden be faced with a different look. They are likely to be feeling a little tense near the end of the set anyway, and this change may make them start thinking too much. That is what you want them to do. While they are pondering the possible causes and effects of this strategy change, they'll be less certain of their own game plan and possibly less decisive in executing it.

In mixed doubles, the female partner of a returner will probably have many balls hit at her when she is at the net. This can be intimidating, but if she is looking for those shots and expecting them to come her way, then she can better handle them. The key to playing at the net, besides expecting balls to come at you, is to watch the opponents intensely to get a clue as to where they will hit it. Keep the racket in front of the body to eliminate a big swing, and don't panic. Another important concept is to use the backhand, not forehand (see figure 5.7), to hit balls that are hit at your body. Any ball on the backhand side, all the way to the right hip, should be hit with the backhand volley.

Here's an advanced player's tip I learned from Frew McMillan, who was a really clever doubles player. When your partner hits a particularly good return of serve that has the opponent stretched out wide to hit a volley, the volleyer would love to see the net player poach so that he or she could just push the ball down the line. The cross-court volley on that wide return is difficult to get away from the net player, who is looking for the ball down the middle. So when the return is hit well, poach some of the time—but do not automatically do so every time or a good team will hit that volley down the line, out of harm's way. On the flip side, when your partner hits a good, firm return right at the incoming volleyer, then you should poach occasionally because the volleyer will not be expecting the move and you will have the element of surprise. The volleyer will begin trying to hit the volley firmly, cross court and deep. This shot, aimed to land deep in the court, will be about shoulder level and is a perfect ball to take out of the air with an interception.

5.7 When playing at the net, handle any balls that are hit at your body with a backhand. Here you see my son Ramsey backhanding a ball that was hit at his right hip.

This is a particularly effective tactic to use in a tight situation such as the one in the following story. I made the finals of the singles and doubles at the US Open in 1971. The semifinals were rained out 3 days in a row, so we played the singles and doubles semis on Tuesday and the finals on Wednesday. Needless to say the finals matches were a bit anticlimactic for everyone involved. The singles final involved four sets that I was able to win. There was a break between the singles and doubles, so the doubles match started in the late afternoon. It got later and later as Erik van Dillen and I went into the 3rd set with a 2–1 lead in sets. Unfortunately we lost the fourth set. Only about 20 minutes of natural light remained, and there were no court lights. We got together with the referee to discuss the situation. Everyone was pretty burnt out by then, and no one wanted to stay until *Thursday* to finish the tournament. So we agreed on a compromise: we would split the prize money and play a 9-point tie-breaker for the title. Talk about pressure! To make a short story shorter, Erik was serving the last 3 points (if needed) at 3–all in the tie-breaker, and on both points he missed his first serve. Our opponents, John Newcombe and Roger Taylor, both hit forehand topspin returns right at my partner, who in the dim light, tried to hit them back toward the returner. The net player poached and hit a winner. Game, set, match, and US Open title to the bad guys.

Remember, the returner's partner is critical to the success of the team, and the role of this player must not be downplayed or overlooked. A good performance by the partner can save the day when the returns are not working, and a bad one can make the returner look really bad despite his or her own great play.

Executing Controlled Volleys and Angles

The game of doubles requires that players use more *feel* and *touch* than they use in singles play. What does this mean? Consider that in doubles there are more options available for volleyers. There are two opponents to work with, and they are likely to be in all sorts of different positions on the court during a point. The goal is to keep your opponents hitting *low* volleys from their toes or to force them to try to hit through you from behind the baseline. If you can do this, then you will have many opportunities to put the ball away from the net. It takes *feel* to control the ball by taking the pace off the opponent's hard shots and directing shots to their feet. Sometimes the words feel and touch are used interchangeably. However, when I discuss

113

feel, I mean the ability to handle power and to change the pace and direction of a shot. I see touch as the result of what occurs with feel—the execution of the delicate shots. I'll discuss how to actually gain better feel with the volleys later in this chapter.

There are three concepts to keep in mind when trying to keep your opponents off balance with touch volleys:

1. **Control of the volley over power.** In doubles harder is not always better. I have seen great teams that rarely hit the ball as hard as they can, even when serving. But these teams have terrific control of their volleying, and this helps them win. I've also seen many teams who seem to think that they can hit their opponents off the court. Good volleyers make such teams hit more shots and wait for them to hit one into the net or out of play. They use the pace of their powerful opponents to hit firm, deep volleys, forcing the opposition to hit another ball from behind the baseline. Today the pros are hitting the ball harder and harder, but those who are successful in doubles don't hit the ball hard unless the right shot presents itself.

2. **Careful placement of the shot.** Whether you are serving or returning, you want to use subtle placement to keep your opponents off balance so that they hit the ball with less control. They will either make mistakes or give you an easy shot to hit. That is how you win in doubles. There is nothing more frustrating for a team than to hit the ball harder or better than the opponents and not be able to win. Keep your opponents frustrated by placing shots that are not comfortable or easy for them to hit. Sometimes good placement is so subtle that the opponents are barely aware of it; they simply notice that they are always reaching a little and can never quite get themselves in the exact position they'd like to be in to hit their shots.

3. **Variety of shot selection.** Using touch volleys successfully involves setting your team up by using variety. This is what sets doubles tennis apart from the game of singles. It makes the game more creative and fun. The big, strong players are not as dominant in doubles as they might be in singles because there is more thinking involved. There is more opportunity to hit different shots and therefore to penetrate the opponents' weaknesses. I have seen many big doubles players react very awkwardly to dinks, lobs, angles, and drives from smaller, less powerful foes. Doubles can be more of a thinking player's game, but you have to have the tools to implement the thoughts that are taking place. The tools to have on hand include deep shots, mid-length balls, angle volleys, and drop shots, all of which you can execute off the same shot from your opponent. I discuss the options for using each of these shots in this chapter.

⬤ Hit the Ball With Feel and Touch

To develop *feel* you need to hold the racket lightly and in front of the body, ready to go to the forehand or backhand. This manner of holding the racket is what people refer to as "soft hands." One way to describe how to do this correctly is that you should use enough pressure on the racket to hold a small bird in your hand so that it could not fly away but not so much that it would hurt the bird. Support the racket with the non-dominant hand at the throat of the racket so that you can maneuver the racket easily in any direction.

I recommend using a continental grip at the net, with only a subtle movement of the palm on the handle to adjust for hitting a forehand versus a backhand volley—the palm moves down and behind the racket on the forehand volley (see figure 6.1*a*), and up and in toward the body on the backhand volley. Regrip the racket with only the last three fingers of the hand, keeping the forefinger and thumb in the same position (see figure 6.1*b*). There is another school of thought that recommends a full change of grip when volleying; I'll admit that some players have been very successful with this method. But keep in mind that the higher the level of the game, the less time there is to make a grip change at the net.

Start with the racket head at about eye level. This allows you to more easily hit slightly downward and to have a slightly open racket face at contact. By

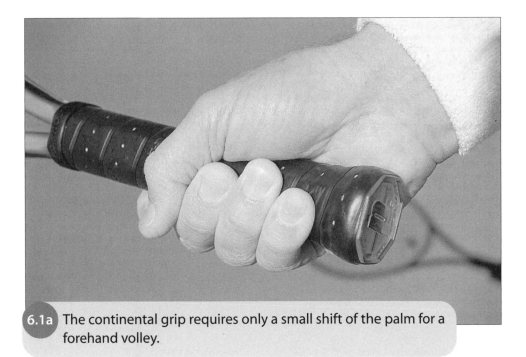

6.1a The continental grip requires only a small shift of the palm for a forehand volley.

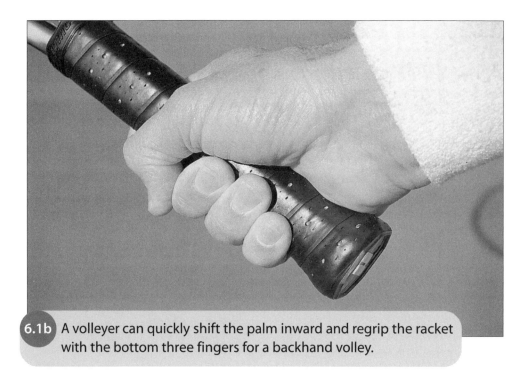

6.1b A volleyer can quickly shift the palm inward and regrip the racket with the bottom three fingers for a backhand volley.

doing these two things, you can impart some underspin on the volley for control and can hit the ball firmly toward your target. If you are hitting a touch volley off a hard shot, let the racket "give" slightly as you hit it (see figure 6.2). This takes the pace off the shot. To hit it hard, squeeze the grip at contact and don't let the racket give. Practicing with these concepts in mind will help you develop a sense of how much to let the racket give depending on what you are trying to do with the volley. Once you have the general idea, the best way to practice touch volleys is to alternately hit one firm, deep volley and one drop shot that dies after it goes over the net. Repeatedly hitting these two extreme volley shots will clarify the difference between hard and soft shots and will enable you to execute both more quickly. In chapter 7, I'll provide some drills to help you vary your volleys and develop feel.

6.2 Using a less rigid grip on the racket produces a softer, slower volley.

Serving Team

Ideally, you serve and volley when you are serving. The key to serving and volleying successfully is to get a high percentage of first serves in and get to the net quickly. The next issue is how you handle the return of serve.

First Volleys

Good players get to the net so quickly that they have to hit very few half-volleys. They hit first volleys inside the service line and before the return bounces (figure 6.3). Hitting a low volley is difficult, and it is hard to get a great deal of power on the shot, but it is better to hit such shots than to have to consistently hit aggressive half-volleys.

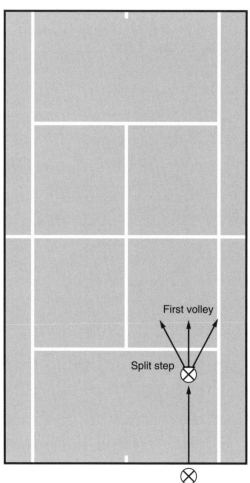

6.3 For the first volley, the server should take two explosive steps and a third slower step to gain control. The server should then split step right as the returner hits the ball. The split step puts the server in balance so that he or she can cut toward the returner and hit the volley inside the service line.

Deep Volley

The first volley should be hit deep into your opponent's court so that he or she has to hit the second shot from behind the baseline (figure 6.4). This is another place where feel comes into play. Taking the hard return of serve and controlling the volley so that the ball hits just inside the baseline requires a special feel. It is better to hit the ball more softly and higher than you'd like, as long as it goes deep, than it is to drill the ball hard and short. It is actually easier for an opponent to hit an aggressive passing shot off a hard and short ball than off a ball that lands near the baseline without much pace on it—and in the latter case, you have more time to get into position for the next shot.

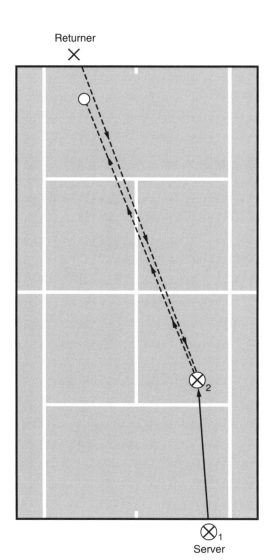

6.4 The deep volley is the basic volley off the return of either the first or the second serve. The goal is to get as close as possible to the net to hit the first deep volley.

Angle Volley

If you can make contact close enough to the net, the little angle volley (figure 6.5) is an option that can confound your opponents. This is a combination of a drop volley and a firm volley. This precise shot is hit soft and short like a drop volley, but it takes the pace off the ball and sends it to the side like an angle volley. When it lands, it runs away from the opponent and off the court. Again, it requires good feel and touch to hit this shot consistently. If you hit this delicate creation a little too hard, it will either go wide or sit up for your opponent to jam down your throat or down the line for an easy winner. I have done this a few times on big points and have gotten a fairly strong reaction from my partner (sometimes verbal, sometimes just loud body language). If you perform this precise little maneuver incorrectly too many times, your partner may become an ex-partner.

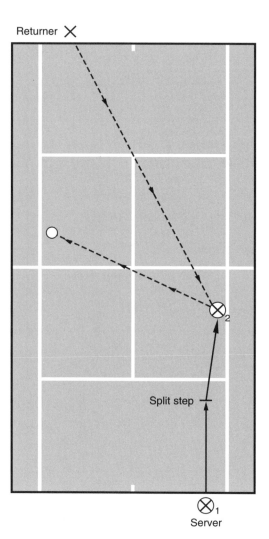

6.5 If you get in close and have a return that is hit near the sideline, the angle volley can be hit as a hard volley off a really high return or as a soft volley or drop shot.

Down-the-Line Volley

Another option for the first volley is the down-the-line volley. This can be hit down and hard from a high, slow, sitting return of serve, or it can be hit as a finesse dink shot that goes right to the net player's feet when the return is low (figure 6.6). This is a good shot to hit when the other team is poaching a lot and you want to either keep them honest or go down the line when the net player moves across. The high return and subsequent banged volley are easy to accomplish. The trick of putting it over the net with no pace and at the opponent's feet requires almost magical skills. You are moving forward very fast to get to the ball before it bounces, and you may be reaching for the return of serve. Great body control and racket control are necessary for this shot. The head must be kept centered and the footwork must be agile in order to maintain balance. The racket must have limited and controlled movement so that the contact point is precise. Great volleyers put the racket in front of the body early so that there is no need to make a big adjustment at the last minute. This way they can just use the hand to redirect the ball as they take the pace off the return.

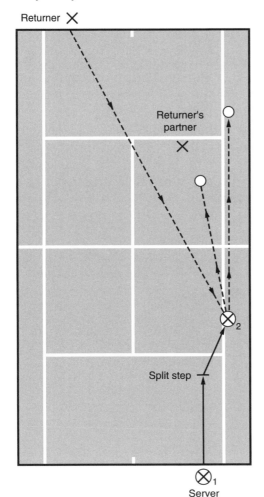

6.6 Whether the down-the-line shot is placed at the net player's feet or near the sideline, it is effective against teams who like to poach.

Half-Volley

There are several issues to consider when deciding whether or not to hit a half-volley in a particular situation. First of all, if you hit the volley, you make contact sooner and closer to the net, which gives your opponent less time to recover from the return of serve and to move to the next shot. Second, the half-volley has to be timed perfectly, which is difficult in light of the different types of spin that your opponents may use. A dipping topspin shot jumps up a bit more than a flat ball, and the slice or chip shot skids a little. The other issue is that when you hit the volley, you swing slightly downward and open the racket face to get the ball over the net. To hit the half-volley, you have to get the racket below the ball with a vertical or closed racket face and brush up as you follow through in order to avoid giving your opponent the chance to put away an easy pop-up. The decision of whether to hit a volley or a half-volley has to be made quickly as you approach the ball so that you can adjust the position and angle of the racket face (see table 6.1).

Some players have a feel for the half-volley and are able to handle the low balls well. Most people who hit this shot well have served and volleyed for a long time and therefore have learned from experience. My old doubles partner, Bob Lutz, had one of the best half-volleys in the game (actually he still does). He was very strong and held the same grip (continental) for both the forehand and the backhand. In fact he held the same grip for all of his shots so that he wouldn't have to think about changing grips for any ball that was swatted at him. The problem was that when his grip was off slightly, it affected every shot that he attempted. It was kind of funny when this happened, but the problem didn't usually last long. He'd make a minor adjustment and be back on top of his game. When Bob came to net, he could use a short backswing to sweep the ball off the short hop and drive it

Table 6.1	
Volley Shot Selection	
Returns	**Volley type**
Drive	Firm, deep
Block	Firm, deep Angle Half-
Chip and charge	Soft, short Angle Half-
High	Various Down-the-line

accurately into the corner. In order to hit this shot, Bob would get down to the ball by bending the front knee and taking a fairly long stride so that the racket head would not drop to the ball but would instead stay more or less parallel to the ground. His wrist was so strong that he could flick the ball down the line at the last minute if the opponents poached. I would literally laugh sometimes when he pulled this off, even though this was not good sportsmanship. A few of the guys would kid Bob that the reason he had such a great half-volley was that he didn't get into the net quickly enough to hit the ball before it bounced and therefore had had more practice at it than anyone else.

When your opponents return the second serve they will usually be more aggressive and therefore force you to volley a ball with a lot of pace. If this is the case, be prepared to control the ball by taking some pace off the shot and guiding it toward the baseline. If the return is hard and high, then it is going out. If the return is high from a block or chip, get it before it bounces and knock it down the line or hit a hard angle volley for a winner. You should be able to get closer to the net on a slow serve unless the opponent takes the ball on the rise and dumps it at your feet. In that case, using the angle volley or the short volley at their feet would be appropriate.

Second Volleys

Once the first volley is hit, the offensive team or serving team should be in control of the net. This is when the volleying team should work together as a unit and shift in the direction that the ball is placed. For example, if the first volley is hit cross court (and hopefully deep), the server's partner should move toward his or her sideline to guard for the down-the-line passing shot. At the same time the server or first volleyer should move toward the centerline. To visualize this positioning, imagine that you and your partner are connected by a 10-foot rope and that the two of you must always keep that rope taut by staying the same distance away from each other. You should follow the ball together so that there is never a big gap between you and so that you are never so close together that the rest of the court is open. When I play against good teams, I often feel that the players are working as a unit and covering the court so well that I have to hit a very low-percentage shot just to have a chance to win the point. If you and your partner stay in good position and volley consistently, then you can put significant pressure on the other team.

The second volley is more likely to be a touch volley. If the serving team is in good position, the opposition is at their mercy. If the receiving team stays back, then the volleyers can hit some short angle volleys to win the point. If the receiving player comes in behind the return, the volleyers' goal is to get the ball down at their opponents' feet to force them to hit up. If the ball is low, you cannot volley hard and direct it at their feet. You must hit it softly at the onrushing players so that the ball will drop soon enough to be a low volley for them. Your target is their shoestrings. It is beautiful to watch a player try to negotiate that low ball and not pop it up to the other team for the kill. If the first volley is not hit as precisely as intended, the game becomes a dogfight.

Roy Emerson–Fred Stolle

One of the great teams of the 1960s was Roy Emerson and Fred Stolle. They were two of the top players to be reckoned with in singles, and when they got together to play doubles they were truly remarkable. "Emmo" gave "Fiery" a couple of lessons in singles in the Wimbledon final, but that didn't seem to affect their ability to pull together and whip most of their doubles foes. In fact they shared a flat during Wimbledon, and Fred cooked breakfast for them each morning, even on the day of the final.

These two Aussies had perfect games for doubles. They were serve and volleyers when they played singles; when they played doubles, they were good servers and great volleyers who also returned serve very consistently and had good instincts for shot selection. They were successful with other partners, but they were most effective when they joined forces.

These right-handers were most impressive. Fred was really solid in all categories of the doubles game, and Emmo could get hot and take over a match with tough shots and quick movement, especially at the net. He would hit the backhand volley from below the net as hard as any player I have ever seen and would almost never miss. Fred and Emmo would put pressure on their opponents by hitting low returns and taking advantage of volleys that were not hit crisply enough. If the competition missed the first serve, Fred would chip and charge, and "stick" the volley if the ball was up in his reach. Emmo could hit the return hard and flat, and could chip and charge as well. His backhand return from the deuce court was as good as they come. If these guys did not come to the net behind their returns, they could hit through, around, or over their opponents on the second shot.

They competed well and enjoyed playing with each other on any surface, no matter what the score. They were tough competitors, but if they lost, they would credit the victors with having played a good match. When they were on top of their game, they rarely had to do this.

These days, when players get floating high shots as they are approaching the net, they sometimes hit swinging volleys instead of concise punch shots. Swinging volleys can be off the forehand or sometimes off the two-handed backhand; they are like a high-swinging groundstroke and are hit with power and topspin.

With the newer, bigger, longer, stronger rackets, this shot can be hit with pretty good control as well as pace. It will usually be a winner or error and the point will be over. In the past I didn't recommend this shot, but now I think it is a good, high-percentage shot if you have practiced it enough.

 Returning Team

As far as volleying, the returning team is in a different situation from the serving team. The volleying technique is the same once the returning team gets to the net, but getting to the net in good volleying position is a challenge. In the following sections, I'll discuss when and how to use lob volleys as well as the scenarios that a returning team may face while trying to get into position at the net to hit the various types of volleys and angles.

The trick for the retuning team is to get into position to execute effective volleys. This may mean shifting toward one side after the first volley, as Ramsey and I did here.

Lob Volley

The lob volley is one of the great finesse shots of all time. It can be either very effective play or virtual suicide. The time to use it is when you are playing against a team that likes to close in dramatically. Usually such a team will have hit a good low shot and will then try to take the net away. It is always fun to see your opponents flying toward the net only to see them have to stop abruptly, look up, and retreat back toward the baseline. If you use the lob successfully a few times, then your opponents will probably come in a little slower and thus allow you to hit the ball at their feet more easily.

That is the good news. If you are just a little bit off in executing the lob volley, you can kiss your . . . partner . . . goodbye. If you strike the ball too softly, and it doesn't get up high enough, then someone can get hurt because you are all so close to each other. I remember getting some meaningful looks and then a few less than complimentary words from Bob Lutz about a case of "lob volleyitis" I developed. I hit a few too many of these touch shots that were not successful, and my doing so cost us some matches. I kept thinking that the lob was going to work, but it didn't, and of course the opponents started to anticipate the shot. The lob volley is a good shot to use if you have the ability to hit it well and if you employ it as a surprise tactic.

One Up and One Back

Generally the point starts with one player at the net and the other one back by the baseline returning the serve. Ideally the player at the baseline is trying to take the net and take charge of the point. If the opposing player does not come to the net behind the return of serve, then the returning team has to assess the quality of the shot. If the return is hit poorly, then the net player has to be ready to move back, reflex the ball, or duck. On the other hand, if the return is hit well, then the net player can close in toward the net and try to intercept the first volley.

As I mentioned in chapter 3, the returning net player should be looking at the opponents to determine what kind of return of serve has been hit. He or she can decide what action to take right away based on the type of serve that was hit. If it is a big serve into the corner, then the net player will probably be thinking defensively. If the first serve is missed, then the net player will hope that his or her partner will make an aggressive return and allow the net player to play more offensively. Now it is also possible that the returner will hit a great return off a sterling first serve or misjudge the ball so badly that he or she is apologizing for it before it gets over the net.

When the net player poaches after a good return, he or she will want to hit a firm volley either down the middle or at the other net player. It will most likely not be a touch volley, but then again it just might be a little angle that takes the other team by surprise or catches them off balance. An example of a situation in which this might occur is if the returner on the deuce side hits a good low return down the middle to the net-rushing server, and the server hits the volley down the middle. When the returner's partner crosses to poach, he or she can hit a forehand angle volley into the alley of the server.

So the returning net player has to be alert, and that is why this position is sometimes referred to as the "hot box." You will either love your returning partner for creating so many opportunities for you to look good, or hate him or her for enabling the opponents to clobber you unmercifully. The one thing that should not be true is that your partner is making bad shots on purpose. If this is the case, then say thanks for playing and goodbye, and move on.

When things aren't going well, you may want to try having both players stay back at the baseline while the opponents serve their first serve. This gives you a chance to get the ball back without leaving your net player too vulnerable. Also it forces the volleyer to hit strong volleys at the baseline without the benefit of a target. This both-back formation should be used only on first serves. The returner's partner should move to the service line on the second serve.

The one up and one back positioning for the returning team should only be temporary, and the back player should be looking fervently for the short ball so the that he or she can move toward the net and get in good position for a point-ending volley. If you stay back because you cannot get the right ball to hit and come in on, then your partner should look for a ball to intercept during the back-court rally. Some teams like to be in this situation because the player at the net is the strong volleyer and the one at the baseline is the good groundstroker. As I said, it is OK to be in this formation temporarily, but you should practice the art of taking the short ball and coming to the net behind it so that your opponents are forced to hit it through, around, or over you.

Sandy Mayer was a good volleyer who would try to come to the net after every return of serve. He was very good at taking the ball on the rise as he was moving forward. When he got hot, the opposition would wind up hitting a lot of balls at their shoestrings only to look up and see him moving toward them.

All Four at the Net

Whether the returners start with both players back or with one up and one back, both players on both teams may get to the net, and the game then resembles dueling pistols at 15 feet. The second volley is when things really happen, and the point often ends with that shot. If the returning team does their job well or the serving team doesn't execute the first volley as well as they'd hoped to, then all four players can end up at the net. Sometimes teams practice trying to take the net away from the team that is there. This is good practice for finesse and feel. You can take the net by hitting hard to encourage the opponents to make a mistake or by chipping a ball low and coming up to the net behind the shot, looking for a high ball. If you don't get the ball low enough, you could get clobbered when you come up to the net. Of course you can throw in a couple of lobs to keep the net players a little further back from the net so that the dink shot or topspin angle has a better chance of getting to their feet.

If the players can keep the ball low and come to the net, four players hitting and reflexing from only 10 to 15 feet apart is what I consider the most exciting situation in the game of tennis. At no other time is the action more fast and furious. This action may contain some reflex volleys off of the odd misplayed high ball, some cat-and-mouse dink shots hoping for a high reply, or some cute little angle shots that keep all four players scrambling and adjusting their positions at the net. This is the time when some of the most extraordinary shots in tennis, such as the around the net post shot I describe later in this chapter, may transpire. This kind of shot happens only a few times in a career, but it sure is fun when it happens.

Angles from groundstrokes and angles from volleys make for some real stretching on the part of the opponents, and the down-the-line shot may be the best option if they are drawn out of position. When an angle is produced, there may be a reply with an even sharper angle. I was involved in an exchange where so much angle had been produced, the ball's movement was almost parallel to the net. This can happen if the opponent anticipates the angle and is therefore ready to run it down. From the wide position off the court, the return angle shot is a good selection, but because the opponent probably expects the angle, the shot down the middle could be the best choice. If the opponent's partner tries to cover the middle, then the shot down the line is the way to go. The other alternative, if both players are closing in to cover the angles, is the quick lob. This is when team experience and, of course, the ability to hit finesse shots become even more valuable. Even though tennis has become more power oriented in recent years, I guarantee that these finesse shots can be as effective as ever against most opponents.

Using the Angles

One reason doubles is so much fun to play is the fact that the court is nine feet wider than the singles court. This creates some very interesting opportunities for the use of *angles*. The extended width of the court geometrically increases the number of angles you can use to try to get your opponents out of position. With a good understanding of the benefits of this extra space, a team can make their foes run more and enjoy the game less.

To give you an example of what a difference this nine feet makes, let me tell you about an experience I had playing a singles exhibition against another

Ellis Ferreira, a great doubles player, demonstrates fine technique on this forward angle volley.

Wimbledon champion. We weren't playing at Wimbledon, and it wasn't exactly a men's singles match. In fact it was a "mixed singles" match, me against the great Evonne Goolagong Cawley from Australia, at Sea Pines Resort on Hilton Head Island. Evonne is younger than me, but that was not the problem. The problem was that we were playing on clay and I was limited to one serve and she could hit the ball into my alleys! This meant that I could not win any free points on my serve without taking a big risk, and that if I didn't hit an offensive shot that went in on the first shot then I was on my way to getting much more exercise than I had bargained for. The good news was that Evonne had spent some 30 years of her life trying *not* to hit in the alleys when playing singles, so it wasn't easy for her to take advantage if the extra width. When she finally got used to the idea of using the 4-1/2 feet on both sides of the singles court, she had a great time with me. The only thing that stopped her occasionally was when she laughed a little too hard as she watched me slide into the side fence running for one of her stupid little angles. That day I learned that the extra width is considerably more than 9 feet when you hit a ball sharply cross court from outside your own alley.

I have seen angles used by some of the best. My longtime partner, Bob Lutz, created the short cross-court backhand angle from nowhere. I even had to clap along with our opponents periodically when, although they knew it was coming, the ball slid past their outstretched rackets. There would seem to be no room for Bob's angle shot in the court, yet it would fit very nicely, from my point of view, time after time.

For the angle to work well, you have to have to receive the right kind of ball from your opponent. The ball has to be a wide shot in order to offer an angle opportunity. In general, a good way to bring about an opportunity to hit an angle is to hit a wide serve. This does not automatically give you a wide ball in return, but it moves your opponents off the court and creates some openings. While the player recovers from hitting the return of serve from the wide serve, you may be able to hit behind him or her with a sharp angle or hit the volley down the middle where there is a hole.

During the rally, there will be opportunities to hit angle shots, especially when you get a ball in your alley or outside the alley. It is fun to take advantage of these situations and get your opponent way off the court. The angle shot will just keep drawing the opponent who is chasing it further and further off the court.

There is one caution you should keep in mind. When you hit a good angle, be aware of your team's positioning after the shot. After you hit the angle, you give your opponents a great chance to hit an even better angle back if they can get to your shot in time to set up. Move together as a team to the side where the shot has been hit to cover the best options that your foes have. But once an extreme angle is hit, it is impossible to cover all the options on a doubles court: the down-the-line shot is dangerous, the shot directed to the middle is available, and the sharp return angle is a possibility. You simply cannot cover all three of these scenarios, as well as the lob, with only two players. The moral of the story is that you need to decide carefully when to hit the angle and strike it well enough so that the opponents will not have time to set up and hurt you with their reply.

It takes a while to get a feel for what an angle can to do for you and how to defend or take advantage of one that is executed against you. But the angle shot certainly brings great variety and interest to the game of doubles. In the 1978 quarterfinals on the center court of Wimbledon, Bob Lutz and I became ensconced in a mighty battle with Bob Hewitt and Frew McMillan. Together, these gentlemen won 10 major titles (French, Wimbledon, and Davis Cup) in doubles and made up one of the great teams of the '70s. We were in the fifth set and behind 9–8 as the sun was going down. It was about 9:30 P.M. and a packed stadium was watching this late show. It was deuce, and we were two points away from losing the match. Bob was at net and hit one of his classic backhand angle volleys; it took Frew off the court and into the cheap seats (actually, there are no cheap seats at Wimbledon, especially not in the front rows). Frew scurried after it and tracked it down just before jumping over the little wall that protects the front row. He slapped the little white ball (this was before the change to yellow balls) from four inches above the ground, down the line, around the net post, into our alley. This a legal shot, and I was ready for it because he had hit the exact same shot for a winner earlier in the match. (A player hitting it twice in one match is more than unusual; this shot may be hit once a year in competition, in a good year, by a professional doubles team.) I popped up the volley from just beyond the service line, and Bob Hewitt hit the sitter with his forehand down the line, missing by about two inches. We were that close to being down match point. We won that game, and the match was suspended for the evening. I wish I could tell you that there was a happy ending to the story. We came back the next day and lost 15–13 in a thrilling, but heartbreaking finish. The only consolation was that it was billed as one on the great confrontations on center court that year. It was an exciting match and a real highlight of my Wimbledon memories, even though we lost the battle.

Angles can be hit a number of different ways. Each of these shots can be produced with various types of speed and spin:

The **topspin angle** can be devastating to your opponents. If it is hit properly and gets by the player at the net, then there is almost no chance of retrieving it. This shot will be struck with quite a bit of racket head speed from below the ball, with a severe low-to-high swing. That makes the ball dip abruptly after it clears the net, and when it hits the ground it will shoot forward. The topspin angle shot has to be hit precisely; the fast racket head is moving more up than forward, so it is easy to mis-hit the ball. Even if it doesn't zip by perfectly for a winner, that dipping ball will be a challenge for your opponents to volley offensively.

The **slow rolling** or **flat angle** is effective when the opponents are really faked out of position. If it is hit in the proper situation, when the opponents are moving or leaning toward the middle of the court, it can just be poked cross court. This is a fun shot to watch, but it is even more fun to hit, because the opponents are left looking hapless and embarrassed.

Another way of hitting the angle is with **underspin**. This chip shot stays low all the way over the net and skids away as it bounces. You should hit this shot with a little more control, and it should not be hit too hard. If you hit the underspin angle shot a little high, you're in big trouble, so be precise. You can move in behind this fairly easily and hopefully get a high volley on which to pounce.

The great thing about doubles is that you can beat your opponents by using touch at the appropriate times rather than having to rely on sheer power. It takes some time around the net to get used to the dinks, angles, and lobs that are so effective in the game. If you are a young player who is just getting serious about the game, I suggest that you play a lot of half-court games in which you don't hit the ball hard but you have to maneuver it around in the service box with control and use different types of spin. If you have been playing for a long time, gradually work touch volleys into your repertoire as you practice and play. Consciously take the pace off some of the shots you hit so that they land at your opponent's feet, forcing him or her to hit up. You will then have the opportunity to put away the balls the opponents hit up—and *that* is the time to use power.

Practicing With a Purpose

The key to improving your doubles performance is to continually work on your areas of weakness, both as an individual and a team. Many players do not assess their initial strengths and weaknesses, and they tend to get frustrated because they are not improving. They may make the same mistakes match after match. The problem is not that these players cannot hit the shots or that they use ineffective strategy, it is simply that they need smart, focused practice to fully develop their physical and mental game.

In this chapter, I outline how to evaluate your play after you and your partner have been playing together for a while and how to plan for an effective practice session. I include drills you can do with your partner, with a coach, and with other players.

Evaluate Your Performance

The best way to begin the process of planning a session is to examine the areas in which you and your partner have been struggling during matches. If possible, have a competent coach help you with this evaluation; a coach or other neutral source can provide fresh insight into your game. Focus on your most recent performances. The evaluation session can take place over a meal or during some other off-court situation that allows sufficient time to go through all the areas of your partnership.

During your evaluation, consider aspects of the game such as warm-up sessions before matches, individual technique, team strategy, movement and conditioning, communication, positioning, attitude, and team chemistry. Once you've identified your areas of weakness, you can use the suggestions given in this chapter to work on them.

Warm-Up

Most players think that the match is the only thing to consider when looking at results. The warm-up session sets the tone for the day, but it is often overlooked when evaluating your performance during matches. Since both partners are trying to get ready to play at their best, it may be difficult to completely satisfy each player's warm-up needs if the two warm up together. One partner may need more time, or want to practice different areas of the game, than the other.

Players at all levels sometimes get confused about the purpose of the warm-up. It is a time to get the muscles loosened up and to hit all the different shots that might be used in the match. It is *not* the time to *work* on your game by hitting a basket of serves, for example, or practicing the serve and volley technique for 20 minutes. That is practice for technique improvement and should be done either after the match or on a day when you are not competing. Some players are so insecure about their quality of play that they leave much of their energy, focus, and enthusiasm on the practice court. By the time they start the match, they are probably *still* insecure about their technique and *tired* as well.

Of course some players, including some of the greatest players to play the game, can ignore this advice with impunity. When Guillermo Vilas was at his best, I saw him warm up for an hour before his French Championship matches, which were played on clay. He was playing only singles in the big tournaments then. His matches were 3- to 5-hour epics, even when he won in straight sets, because he was a human backboard and almost never came to the net. One day I asked his coach, Ion Tiriac, why Vilas was warming up so long before his matches. I was particularly curious because he would practice groundstrokes for 45 minutes, then he hit a couple of serves and a few volleys for the other 15 minutes. Tiriac said that Vilas didn't feel ready unless he had worked up a good sweat and had hit enough balls (different shots, or the same shot enough times). I certainly could not argue with the results at the tournament. Vilas won the most physically demanding tournament in the world easily, winning at least one 6–0 set in every match (and spanking yours truly in the process!). After each match he would run about five miles, then go into the locker room and do about 100 sit-ups and 100 push-ups. Sometimes his opponent would still be in the locker room, having been demolished on the court, and would get to see him come in and do these postmatch exercises. In those days he was by far the fittest man on the tour. If you can run and hit all day, then maybe you can warm up for a long time and still play well, but most players are not able to do this and should save their energy and strength for the competition.

Generally you should warm up for 30 to 40 minutes before a doubles match, a bit longer than you would warm up for a singles match. Before actually picking up a racket or hitting a ball, you should first warm up the muscles, get your heart rate up, and break a sweat with 5 to 10 minutes of gentle aerobic activity. Start by jogging around the court at least four or five times, working in some forward running, backward running, side shuffling (both ways), carioca stepping, high-knee running, and rear-kick running as you go.

After you have increased your heart rate, spend 10 minutes stretching all the major muscles of the body including the calves, Achilles tendons, quadriceps, hamstrings, abdominal and back muscles, shoulders, forearms, and wrists.

Spending 15 to 20 minutes doing these aerobic and stretching activities gives you the best preparation for a good practice or match and will help you prevent injury. You have only to spend a few weeks or months in rehab after an injury to realize that this small amount of time spent warming up the body is extremely worthwhile.

Once you have completed the aerobic and stretching component of your warm-up, spend 15 to 20 minutes on the court hitting shots to prepare you for the match. Consider which shots you are most likely to encounter during the match. For example, you need to hit groundstokes for a while, but you'll likely have a limited number of points in which both players are in the back court exchanging groundstrokes. Generally during a doubles match, one player will be back and the others at net, or all four players will be at the net. Therefore it makes sense to spend more time practicing for those situations during the warm-up. After a few minutes of groundstroke exchanges one partner should come to the net and hit volleys for five minutes, then the partners should switch positions. While you're at the net, make sure you each hit lobs and overheads. Then hit some serves and get into some diagonal serve-and-volley points for 5 to 10 minutes. Finish with some volley exchanges, with both of you at the net, to sharpen your reflexes and work on your angle and dink shots. If your partner needs to hit more shots and you are ready to go, see if someone else will step in. Maybe the coach, or another competitor who also wants to hit a few more balls, can go out on the court and do the honors.

Once you have warmed up to play, you will have five minutes on the match court with your opponents just prior to starting the match; this allows for last-minute hitting to get you ready for battle. This time is not so much for warming up the body as it is for getting used to the immediate conditions, the court itself, and possibly the crowd in attendance. Keep in mind during these five minutes that you are warming up with the enemy; thus these are not the folks you want to ask for cooperation in practicing those shots you are struggling with. I have seen many players innocently tell their opponents, "I'd like to work on a few more volleys or backhands." This kind of statement immediately sends up a red flag signaling to savvy players that these are the shots the speaker is especially concerned about, or that this player is trying to confuse the opponents. I have sometimes seen players refuse to cooperate with their opponents during this practice time in order to prevent them from being fully prepared for the match. This is poor sportsmanship and unacceptable behavior.

A better warm-up routine may greatly improve your play at the start of your matches, and the way you start your matches may dictate the way you continue to play. Your opponents won't have the extra confidence that comes with starting off well, and you will not have the pressure that comes with starting off poorly.

This warm-up routine is something you will want to do before every match, if not before every practice session. You can vary the routine a bit to suit your needs. If you want to concentrate on a specific shot or doubles situation during practice, you may prefer to just do the aerobic and stretching part of warm-up and a little hitting, then go right into hitting those shots you want to practice. It is a good idea to work on problems with technique early in your practice session, when you are fresh. You will likely be more intense and productive, both physically and mentally, and your attitude will be more positive. If you work on technique at the end of a practice, you will probably be too fatigued to get much out of the practice and may even ingrain some bad habits.

Technique

Improper or poor technique may be your biggest weakness. Some problems may be obvious to you or to players who watch you. Criticism may be difficult for you to hear; you may disagree or get defensive when others talk to you about a particular weakness. Try to keep in mind that welcoming critical feedback may be the best way to improve your game. It is helpful if both team members feel that they are working together and that they each

Proper technique is the key to delivering a solid overhead shot.

have areas to improve; this will encourage them to be honest but diplomatic with one another. A respected coach sitting in on the conversation and voicing an objective opinion can lessen a player's sensitivity to feedback. Keep in mind that technical criticism is objective, and it does not reflect on a player's effort, talent, or self-worth. Technique is an area that *can* be improved with practice, so any weakness should be considered a temporary problem that can be resolved with a realistic solution. Keep in mind that there may be more than one way to hit a ball effectively, and that some allowance for individual style should be made. However, the key elements of technique are the same for most good players. These include adopting the proper racket position just before contact and maintaining good balance.

Be sure to assess the following aspects of your technique and to note any areas in which you need to improve:

- Grips
- Ready position of the body
- Ready position of the racket
- Preparation for the hit—backswing
- Preparation for the hit—footwork
- Contact point
- Balance—weight transfer
- Balance—rhythm
- Followthrough
- Recovery

Improving your technique takes a serious commitment. Much thought and a great deal of time are required, first to erase improper muscle memory and then to learn the new technique. It takes several hours of using the correct movements to establish even a minor change well enough to be able to use it automatically in a match situation. Early in the process, it is usually very difficult to tell whether or not you are using the changed technique; you can't see what you are doing and your execution may feel right when it is still wrong. In fact, this is normally the case. To make a change quickly, rely on feedback from others in the initial stages to make sure that you are indeed hitting the ball correctly. With solid, objective feedback from a coach and or a videotape, a change can be made successfully even by a player who has been playing with a bad habit for a long time.

It is best to work on a change in technique when you are not under pressure to play in competitive matches. Try to make a major change during the off-season so that you do not have to use the new shot in a match situation until you have mastered it. A major change such as improving your serving motion with a different toss, changing your grip from Eastern to continental, or using a much greater shoulder turn on the backswing will take a few months to effectively modify. The process of making the change may be a little frustrating, but in time you will progress from feeling uncomfortable with the change to mentally grasping the motion, from occasionally hitting it right to hitting it well in practice but not always in a match, and finally, to hitting it consistently in a match.

If you are making a minor correction—such as bending your knees a little more on a groundstroke, putting a little more underspin on a volley, or watching the ball a little longer on the serve—you may be able put the new technique into action pretty quickly with just a few repetitions. While you are making a minor change you can still play, but you must have patience with yourself as you play and keep your expectations low until the change becomes automatic. Many minor changes are really just "refreshers" in which the goal is to reinstate good technique that has slipped a little over time. The old habit might rear its ugly head at the most inopportune times. If you and your partner understand this, then you will know what to expect and can realistically estimate how long it will take to achieve the desired result.

It is important to have the right attitude about making a change. Good players are not afraid to make a change and understand that it is fun to see the long-term benefits of the improvements. You cannot reach your potential if you are stubborn about trying something new that will help your game and consequently your team's results. If your coach cannot convince you that the change is beneficial then you will find it very difficult to commit to the concept and change your behavior. Keep an open mind, and work through the process of evaluating how the change will improve your overall game. Consider whether the change will have any negative consequences, and be prepared to deal with them.

As a college player, I was constantly improving, but naturally not as quickly as I wanted to. I had won the National Junior Championship, but I still had plenty of room for further improvement. My coach, George Toley at USC, watched me play for a whole year, then finally said to me, "I thought your forehand would develop better than it has because you are a good athlete and have a pretty good feel for the ball, but it hasn't come along as I thought it would." I agreed and was open to his suggestions. Remember that the first and most necessary step in making a change is to buy into the fact that there is a need for change; you must trust that the coach or partner who is helping you assess your weaknesses knows what he or she is talking about. My coach suggested two ways to improve my forehand. First, he suggested that rather than being so rigid with my hand and wrist, I work on being more relaxed. Second, he suggested that I brush up on the ball to get a little more topspin in order to feel the ball better and gain a little more control. I tried to exaggerate the relaxed feeling and to brush up on the ball, and I practiced my forehand for hours upon hours. Becoming more relaxed was a particularly hard change to make. With any kind of change, there is a danger of becoming a little too studied and mechanical during the early part of the process. Since that was the heart of the problem with my forehand, I had to play mental games to let myself go a little more. After several weeks I became more confident with my improved forehand, and I not only hit the ball with more control but also with more power.

Team Strategy

Team strategy is another important area to evaluate. I have seen individuals who have great technique who either do not understand how to play doubles or simply can't work together as a team. That is why I think playing together for a long time does not necessarily make a good doubles team. If your individual style of play conflicts with the requirements for playing doubles, or if your concept of doubles strategy is wrong, then you will never be a good doubles player regardless of how long you stay with your partner.

There was a player who was number one in singles in the United States in the 1970s named Cliff Richey. As I discussed in chapter 1, his style of play was very effective in singles, but it did not suit the doubles game very well; he won by serving and staying back, and then occasionally coming to the net on a good approach shot. When he played singles, he did not feel comfortable coming to the net after every serve. His volley technique was pretty good, but it was not suited for doubles, where it is helpful to take the pace off the ball sometimes as you hit little dink shots and angles. He would usually try to hit the volley deep into the opposite corner and then close in to put the ball away. His return of serve game was effective in singles, but he did not like having to hit the ball into one-half of the court as he was required to do in doubles. Lacking both a big serve and an appropriate return of serve for doubles, he was not very effective on the doubles court.

Richey's other limitation was that, as a young player, he did not care about doubles and therefore didn't play it much. By the time he played at the pro level, he had not developed as great an understanding of doubles strategy as most other players. Many of his competitors had less talent, but they had played doubles all of their lives. Apart from these other factors, Cliff did not really enjoy playing doubles, so he never gave himself a chance to become as good as he might have been.

Bjorn Borg, perhaps the best singles player of all time, was also less effective (though still good) at doubles. He was a five-time Wimbledon Champion and a six-time French Open champ in singles. Even though he won Wimbledon on grass, which suits an aggressive player, Bjorn was a counterpuncher who sometimes played matches in which he rarely made an error. He relied on staying at the baseline, getting every ball back, and passing his opponent when he came to the net. He almost never played doubles except in Davis Cup matches and therefore did not have the best instincts for the game.

To play winning doubles, players must rely on solid team strategy as well as their individual talent and technique. Here the poach is on, and an angle volley will probably win the point.

Bob Lutz and I played Borg in a very important Davis Cup match in Göteburg, Sweden in 1978. It was one match all, after Borg had beaten Vitas Gerulaitis in the first match and Arthur Ashe had beaten Sweden's second singles player, Kjell Johannson. Bob and I figured that we had to win the doubles match and Gerulaitis the other singles match on the third day; Borg was so hot that we were not confident that Arthur could win the last match. We got behind two sets to one to Borg and Ove Bengtson, and we were not looking good. Borg was making every return and not missing any volleys. We had counted on him to be the weak link. Even though he didn't play much doubles, he was such a great champion that he did well by just playing good, high-percentage tennis. He forced us to raise our game, and we were lucky to win in five sets. Besides being one of the great singles champions of all time, Borg had a few things going for him as a doubles player: he had a good serve and got in a high percentage of first serves, he had a great return of serve that made us hit a lot of tough first volleys, and he didn't miss many easy volleys. If we pressured him with really good returns, though, he was in trouble because he didn't have much experience in diving for volleys or in deciding where to hit volleys when his opponents poached.

In this Davis Cup match, Bob Lutz and I were able to play more aggressively and turn the match around to win in five sets. Ove Bengtson turned out to be the weakest link by the end of the match; I think he felt that he had to play better to support Borg in order to win the match and therefore may have pressed too hard.

The best way to work on team strategy is to have a coach watch you play a friendly practice match and evaluate your shot selection as you play (see table 7.1 here; also see table 1.2 on page 8). If you play on a USTA League team and the same coach handles more than one doubles team, he or she can work with two teams at the same time. The coach may have one team try to play a certain way to improve specific areas of team strategy. This is a cooperative effort for all four players; each team and player must contribute, and each can benefit. If the coach has seen you play enough, he or she may have two or three new concepts in mind for you to put into play. You may have all the shots for good doubles, but may not be hitting the right shots at the right time. With a coach on the court periodically giving you advice during your play, you immediately receive input that directly relates to the situation you have just been in. You can experiment with new positioning or shot selection and test the effectiveness of your changes right then and there. It is amazing how quickly you can understand and adopt a new concept by trying it out on the court as opposed to just theorizing about it off the court.

Another great idea for analyzing team strategy is to study a video of a match. This really helps a team see what happened and where improvements can be made in shot selection and positioning. You can stop the video at important frames and view a shot any number of times to decide whether and how you might have approached a point differently. It can be helpful to get an expert opinion from a coach as you view it.

Table 7.1

Troubleshooting Team Strategy

Ask yourself the following questions to assess and troubleshoot your team strategies, or have a coach or another player watch your team and fill out this questionnaire.

Serving

1. Are you missing too many first serves?
2. Do you serve too hard and use too little spin?
3. Do you concentrate enough on your first serve?
4. Do you rush through your first serve?
5. Are your opponents returning your serves consistently and effectively?
6. Are you serving to the proper location and using the proper spin and pace?
7. Should you serve from a different position on the baseline?
8. Should the net player try a different position? (Should the team use the Australian-formation or the I-formation?)
9. Are you poaching too little or too much?
10. Do your overall serving weaknesses seem to be due to technique or tactics?

Returning serve

1. Is your positioning too close, too far back, or too far to one side?
2. Is your shot selection (drive, chip and charge, block) on the return ineffective with most opponents?
3. Do you lob too much or not enough?
4. Should you drive at the net player more?
5. Are your opponents poaching effectively?
6. Should you be more conservative on the first return of serve?
7. Should you be more aggressive on the second return of serve?
8. Should you and your partner sometimes both stay back on first serves?

During points

1. Are you using high-percentage shots or shots that are unlikely to be successful in the given situation?
2. Can you lob more to keep opponents further from the net?
3. Are you volleying too hard, or using too many angle volleys or lob volleys?
4. Do you set up the down-the-middle shots with angles and a variety of shots?
5. Do you move as a team to cover your opponents' shots?
6. Are you playing too aggressively or too conservatively?

Movement and Overall Conditioning

One big difference between tennis and golf is that you cannot ride in a cart between shots while playing tennis. Some fanatical tennis players don't even consider golf a real sport. They think of golf as an activity much like playing billiards, only with different sticks! In tennis the ball is always moving, and a good team will certainly *not* try to hit the ball *back to you* so that you won't have to move.

As I mentioned in chapter 1, one of the directives that the sports medicine committee of the USTA has given is that people should not play tennis to get fit, but should get fit to play tennis. The better the shape you are in, the better and longer you will be able play and the less likely it is that you will be injured. No matter what level you play, even if you only play doubles, it is helpful to try to improve your fitness. Doing so is likely to increase both your mobility and your stamina on the court.

The USTA has developed some tests for players to evaluate their strengths and weaknesses. These involve quickness, explosiveness, speed endurance, strength, and recovery. The tests can be found in the book *Complete Conditioning for Tennis* by the USTA (Human Kinetics, 1998).

The real test of fitness is whether you can play at your best level for three full sets one day, do the same thing the following day, and not get injured in the process. Some injuries are the result of freak accidents, such as a player running into the fence and spraining a wrist or ankle. Other injuries are chronic injuries and overuse injuries caused by a lack of muscle strength or flexibility. Players can prevent many injuries by doing a complete warm-up, using proper technique, and building enough strength and flexibility to last through long matches.

When I was in college, we would always start the fall season by doing a lot of work on general conditioning and not playing quite as much. The coach wanted us to peak at the end of the season for the NCAA Championships. Other teams would hit balls for hours and hours early in their season, and they would end up getting hurt or burnt-out by the time the big dance (the championships) came around. We, on the other hand, would start our practice during the first three or four weeks by going to a nearby track and doing calisthenics, some stretching, and then a two- or three-mile run. After a few weeks, we would not run distances, but wind sprints. After about a month of emphasizing this buildup in conditioning, we would spend most of our time on the court, with periodic conditioning to maintain the fitness level that we had achieved. By the end of this time we felt strong and fit. This routine gave us a good physical base for going all out in our tennis. Our coach, George Toley, must have been doing something right because he won 10 NCAA team titles and his players won numerous individual singles and doubles titles.

It has been proven that tennis is both an anaerobic and an aerobic sport. That is, during a match you are required to run and move throughout the match (aerobic activity) with breaks in between points, and you must use strength and bursts of power to hit the ball (anaerobic activity). The results of analyses done on a typical tennis match are amazing. Depending on the surface and style of play, only a small percentage of actual time is spent moving and hitting the ball during a match. It can be less than 10 percent of the actual time on the court. The rest of the time is spent recovering from the previous point and preparing for the next point (up to 25 seconds between points, 90 seconds on changes of end, and 2 minutes at the end of a set). The time the ball is in play requires explosive movement, either on the baseline or toward the net. Even though the movement is not constant during a long 3- or 5-set match like it is during a marathon run, a player's aerobic capacity can be dramatically tested because of the total amount of time on the court and the need to recover 100 percent before the next match. Ideally, you want to recover well enough to play effectively even after several long consecutive points. Smart players will take the full 25 seconds after long points so that they can recover as fully as possible before the next point.

It is a good idea to get into relatively good aerobic shape by doing two to three miles of running each day before the season, as we did at USC. What being in decent shape means is relative, depending on your level of play. If you are playing in league matches every week and competing every weekend, you can evaluate how well you are recovering between matches. If you are losing your stamina or not getting to balls at the end of match or feeling low on energy, then you have to work on conditioning. Once you are in decent shape, then you can work on conditioning that will directly enhance your explosiveness and quickness. Tennis is a game of quick stops and starts, not one of constant low-speed movement. Therefore, doing a lot of long-distance running, say more than three miles a day, beyond the first few weeks of training would be detrimental to your effectiveness because you would be developing the slow-twitch muscles too much and not developing the fast-twitch muscles that are so very important to the quick movement required in tennis.

To improve your on-court movement or mobility, you need to increase your power, which is the combination of strength and speed. Improving this anaerobic aspect of play will enable you to be stronger longer. You should also work on reaction time and quickness. Flexibility is also important to improve your performance and decrease your chance for injury. There are tests that you can do on the court to evaluate your power, quickness, and flexibility. These tests can also be found in the book *Complete Conditioning for Tennis* by the USTA (Human Kinetics, 1998). There are drills given at the end of this chapter that you can do on and off the court to improve your performance in these areas.

Positioning

You can evaluate your positioning by videotaping a match. Shoot the video from high behind the court, if possible, so that you can see the whole court on the screen. This way you can see the position of every player throughout the point. Of course, professionals who play a televised match may be able to get a copy of the match from the production team that has the added benefit of the expert commentator's analysis. The great thing about using a video is that the players can see for themselves where and when mistakes occur and can see the consequences of those mistakes. The coach can point out possible changes that could improve the play in future matches and show how the changes would make a difference. It is easier for some people to understand the problem and the recommended solution through visual means than to just hear a suggestion from a coach and imagine how it might help. The video is a great teaching tool, and it has benefited many teams. Table 7.2 provides a checklist for evaluating positioning.

Over the years, I have had the opportunity to review some of my doubles matches on video. What has benefited me the most from watching these videos is seeing how our team's position on the court affects the way the court looks to the opposing players. It was clear that the closer I was to the net, the less space there was for the opponents to hit. If the opponents didn't lob, then I was very effective playing close to the net. I also noticed that I would sometimes come too far inside the baseline after my split step on the return of serve and get jammed by the serve.

While watching a video of one match, I learned what the returner had been doing when I tossed the ball on the serve. He would change position during the toss. It was hard for me to see this change while playing, but the video made it clear. The next time we played this team, I wasn't thrown off by this player's change of position.

Another way to work on positioning is to play a practice match with a friendly team that will cooperate with you and your coach by allowing the coach to stop play periodically to critique a point and make a suggestion as to the positioning during that point. The emphasis of the coach's input would be on general improvements in positioning and not on how to beat the other team. The coach could help both teams during the practice session so that the experience would be a learning opportunity for everyone.

This practice-match scenario gives a team the opportunity to experiment with different types of positioning and to get a feel for how positioning affects other teams in general. This is certainly the time to try something new. There is no real risk in doing so, and it prevents you from having to try something for the first time during a competitive match. It is important not

Table 7.2
Positioning Assessment for Video Viewing and Coach Evaluation
Server
1. Did you serve from the same position or from a variety of positions along the baseline?
_____

2. Was your serving position effective or could it be more effective for certain opponents?

_____

3. What was your position on the big points, 30–40, 35–40, and 40–30?

_____

Net Player

1. Was your positioning effective overall?

_____

2. Were you able to poach from your position?

_____

3. Did any returns get past you?

_____

4. Were you ever too close to the net and vulnerable to lob returns?

_____

5. Did you move with your partner during the point?

_____

Returner

1. Did your position enable you to return serves with your forehand and backhand with equal ease?

_____

2. Did you change position if the one you were using was not successful?

_____

3. Did you change position on the second serve?

_____

4. Which positions were most effective for you? Why?

_____

Returner's Partner

1. Were you too close or too far back?

_____

2. Did you adjust to the return of serve well?

_____

3. Were you too close to the center or alley?

_____

4. Should you have stayed back with your partner?

_____

to worry too much about the results of this type of practice match. You may not be successful at first with both players staying back on the return of serve, for example, or with trying to return serve and come to the net behind the return. But the more you practice new ideas, the more effective you will be and the better you will understand the effect of different positioning and strategy on your opponents. As I discussed in chapter 4, players can try the Australian formation or the I-formation, crowding the service line or standing way behind the baseline, moving way over to favor the forehand on the second serve return, serving from the alley on the ad court, standing closer or further from the net when their partner is serving, and many other formations. Do not be afraid to try some different positions. The more you try them, the more comfortable you will be using them, when appropriate, in a big match or an important point.

Attitude

Many matches and tournaments are won and lost based on attitude. The best players with the best strokes, best conditioning, best equipment, and best coach do not always win. Sometimes the team with the best attitude wins the match, especially if it's a close one. A match will have its own momentum, which ebbs and flows. If a team gets too caught up in the low points of the match, they may never allow themselves to get into position to reach the ultimate high point—winning. I have seen teams that just refuse to allow themselves to get too discouraged about losing the serve or getting a bad break. They always believe that they can turn the match around. Players can support each other and emphasize the good things that are happening rather than dwell on the bad things. This helps them to feel better and to play better.

Positive attitude is easier said than done. And attitude is sometimes hard to evaluate without some outside help. It is reflected in what is done on the court, as well as what is said on the court. Body language is key. It leads the verbal. In most cases, if the body language becomes negative, then the verbal is soon to follow. The best way to analyze this area, as with positioning and strategy, is viewing the action in a video. I have had people claim that there was "no way" they did or said something negative on the court. Well, that's when we'd "go to the video." They could not refute what was on the screen, and in many cases they were dumbfounded by what they saw. Just as with gambling or a drinking addiction, the first course of action is to get the player to admit that their attitude is hurting them. The video provides a tool to start the attitude rehabilitation process. Unchecked, the slumped shoulders, the shaking of the head, and the raising of the eyes, can lead to name-calling, whining, bouncing the racket, and other damaging verbal and nonverbal behavior.

Experiment and perfect a new formation in practice so that you can implement it in match play with confidence. This is a modified I-formation.

Martina Navratilova–Pam Shriver

These two women from different parts of the world joined forces and dominated the women's game for several years. Martina, a lefty, was born a Czech citizen and later became a citizen of the United States. Pam, a tall right-hander, was a young American star who reached the finals of the US Open singles at the age of 16. Ironically, she lost to Martina in that match.

They got along well on and off the court and formed an aggressive team. Martina became one of the greatest singles players of all time, but, like John McEnroe, her doubles abilities were even better. She started off a little roly-poly, but she later became one of the fittest players on tour, man or woman. She loved to serve and volley and was very athletic, so her style was perfect for the game of doubles.

Pam would slice the ball on the forehand and the backhand. Since she was rangy, she was able to take advantage of Martina's good, low returns of serve. Pam had a good slice serve and a good grasp of the game of doubles. Although she soon became known as "Martina's partner," this was a little unfair. She was a very smart and competitive player who came through for the team in a big way most of the time.

Both women were good servers, and both volleyed very effectively. They would try to intimidate their opponents by moving at the net, whether they were serving or returning serve. It was tough to lob them because Pam was tall and Martina was able to get to any ball. Both players would hit forehands on second-serve returns of serve whenever they had a chance; their opponents had to get a high percentage of first serves in or expect a low return at their feet. Sooner or later Martina and Pam would get enough tough returns in to break serve. The task for their opponents was to try to break serve in order to stay in the match.

They were a fiery team, and their competitiveness enabled them to pick each other up when things got tough. I think their attitude also intimidated their opponents.

Martina retired and then came back to play only doubles on the tour when she was in her late 30s; even at that age she was a force to be reckoned with. The younger players were amazed at how athletic she still was and at her understanding of how to play winning doubles.

Team Chemistry

Team chemistry can be something of a mystery. There's no special quality that ensures that two players will gel as a team. If there is a problem with chemistry, you must communicate with your partner about it. You and your partner don't have to be a perfect match to work well together—even successful marriages have periods of disagreement and friction when things are somewhat heated around the home. Issues of behavior or style of play, with a little discussion, can often be ironed out. Common ground can be discovered. I have seen two guys with diametrically opposed personalities get along pretty well on the court and have tremendous success as a team. One or both of these players will usually need to make an adjustment to make the partnership work. Because these players are willing to make adjustments and share a give and take attitude, this kind of team can be even stronger than an apparently well-matched team. If each player knows his or her role and each player's expectations are met, the couple can do very well together.

Newcombe and Roche were one doubles team made up of two very different personalities. Newcombe is very outgoing and enjoyed being in the limelight. Roche is quiet and solid, and didn't like drawing attention to himself or making a big deal of his success. They understood each other's personalities and roles, and they were one of the best teams ever. As it turned out later, Newcombe became the Australian Davis Cup Captain and Roche was the coach. They worked their magic again together in the late 1990s by leading the Aussies in winning the coveted Davis Cup.

Sometimes a team is just not meant to be. If, despite attempts to accommodate each other, the players' personalities do not mix well, especially in the heat of battle, it may be best for them to split up. It is not worth trying to force a partnership when it is apparent that the chemistry is simply not there. It is best in the long run for both players to try to find someone more compatible.

Plan Your Practice

It is important to have a practice plan that will give you a chance to work on your overall conditioning, technique, and strategy along with your match play. This plan may include time to test new equipment such as different rackets, strings, and shoes. It also might be the time to work out with a new partner and test your compatibility. The percentage of time you spend on each of these components depends on the phase of your training year: preseason, early season, inseason (when your peak competitions are), and off-season (see table 7.3).

The preseason is the time to work on major technique changes, such as changes in grip or stroke changes that take some time. Your expectations of playing well during the preseason should not be too high. Do not play any important competitions during this period; doing so would only be frustrating. As I mentioned earlier in this chapter, the learning process will involve

Table 7.3

Tennis Practice

Phase	Time	Conditioning	Technique	Strategy	Match play
Preseason	4 weeks	15%	60%	15%	10%
Early season	4 weeks	40%	30%	15%	15%
Inseason	4 weeks	10%	20%	30%	40%
Off-season*	4 weeks	50%	50%		

* The off-season is mostly devoted to rest, but when you are practicing, devote half of your time to overall conditioning and half to technique work.

an up-and-down kind of experience, in which you will progress slowly and inconsistently. You may initially think you will never get the new technique down; next you may enter a period where you get it for a while and then lose it. With persistence, you'll be able to make the change work reliably in practice but not in a match. Finally, you'll be able to make it work in a match situation (most of the time).

The early season should involve continued work on technique but also a conditioning component in which you work on your aerobic base and also your anaerobic development. This is the time to really get in shape, having taken some time after your last competitive season and having experimented with any major technique changes during the preseason. Don't worry about strategy too much during this stage. A favorite early season drill used by the pros is the two-on-one drill, in which one player is at the baseline and two are at the net, or one player is at the net and two are at the baseline. The two players who are positioned together keep feeding balls constantly, using a bucket of balls to fire shots across the net until the one player is exhausted. That player tries to hit shots that he or she would likely hit while playing doubles. This drill is particularly good for working on net play, which is so important for doubles. Some on-court drills allow you to work on technique and conditioning while competing to win the most points; others can be done without worrying about winning or losing. Off-court conditioning exercises such as lunges, sprints, jumping rope, calisthenics, and side shuffles are also important in getting your body in shape to play. The USTA's *Complete Conditioning for Tennis* (Human Kinetics, 1998) provides a comprehensive training program for overall conditioning for tennis. Cross-training by participating in another sport such as basketball, Frisbee football, soccer, or cycling is a fun way to get in shape, but remember, these activities pose the risk of possible injury, so it is important to warm up and stretch prior to and after participating.

The inseason is the time to concentrate on strategy and playing at your best. Continue to spend a small amount of time maintaining your level of conditioning, and work on fine-tuning your technique with on-court drills. Review and evaluate your play and your competitive skills. Preparing in every way is the key to becoming successful; having done so, win or lose, you can walk off the court after a match knowing that you have given yourself the chance to play your best.

The off-season is the time to put down your racket and get away from the game for a while. This respite is necessary and should not be disregarded, even by the most committed and avid players. It is a time for refreshing yourself, mentally and physically, and maybe for letting some minor injuries heal up. After a period of time away from the game, you should be eager and ready to get back to playing.

Drills for the Team

There are many drills doubles partners can do without another team. Doubles teams on the pro tour warm up by having one team member play the other, and after the match or on a day off partners often work out against each other, emphasizing the doubles tactics that they are trying to improve.

I would say that the majority of the points end, on almost any level of play, after the serve or the return of serve. Certainly 75 percent of doubles points are settled within the first three strikes of the ball. This means that the best way to improve your doubles play is for you and your partner to concentrate on helping each other with the serve and return of serve.

The server must work on both first and second serves. The returner should work many different areas of his or her game, and the server can accommodate the returner by serving in such a way as to allow him or her to hit the types of returns that have proved troublesome. If the returner is having problems with the backhand return, the server can serve exclusively to that side so that the returner knows where the ball is going and can try to groove the shot. Improvement will come much more quickly this way than it would if the returner just played random points.

The areas that the returner should drill include blocking, chipping and charging, and driving. The player may want to learn to return and come to the net after the return; he or she can practice this by having the server hit the serves to a particular spot. The returner may want to focus on attacking second serves with an aggressive return of serve or on developing the forehand return of serve by running around the backhand to hit the second serve. This is a good time to practice different positioning on the first serve in order to get more first serve returns back in play.

To practice chipping and charging behind the return of serve, the returner should hit a return of serve low to the onrushing server's feet while charging toward to net; this requires the returner to control the ball accurately and usually to take some pace off the ball while moving forward quickly. When both of the players and the ball are moving forward rapidly, they must have great body control along with great racket control. The split step before each shot will help the player to consistently maintain good balance. It takes some time to learn to chip and charge effectively.

Returners should also practice the lob when receiving those big serves. It is better to make the opponents hit an overhead, even an easy one, than to miss too many returns of serve.

Second Serve Only

This drill helps the server get used to hitting good second serves consistently and also helps each player play more points out.

1. Players get into position, one on each side of the net.
2. The two play points, with the server hitting only second serves each point.
3. The returner hits each serve back and plays out the point.
4. The server and returner play to 10 points, then switch sides.

First Serve, Second Serve

This drill focuses on serving practice to allow the player to get used to the rhythm of serving a first serve and then a second serve. This drill can be done individually.

1. The server gets into position to serve.
2. The server decides which deuce- and adside targets to aim for during serves.
3. The server hits the first serve to the deuce-side target.
4. The server hits the second serve to the deuce-side target
5. Repeat the drill, with the server hitting first and second serves to the ad-side target.

General Point Simulation

This is a typical doubles drill. One player serves to the other, and the two play out the point cross court much as they would during a match.

1. Players get into position, one on each side of the net.
2. The server executes various types of serves from various positions on the baseline.
3. The server follows each serve to the net as he or she would in a match.
4. The returner hits returns back at the server, varying the type of return.
5. The server volleys cross court back to the returner.
6. Server and returner play out the point cross court.
7. Each player should occasionally hit down the line to practice this shot.

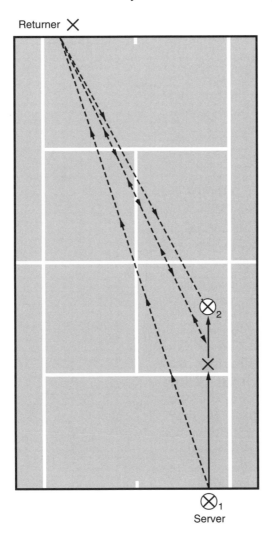

Big Serve and Quick Close

If the server is working specifically on the big first serve followed by quick movement to the net to volley, then he or she should serve hard and come in fast to hit the volley inside the service line, if possible. The server can let his or her partner know where the serve is going so that that the returner has a better chance of getting the return back. If the partner is having trouble returning the serve, then he or she can feed a ball from the place the return would come from, at about the time the return would be hit. This gives the return of serve player more confidence and gives the server more opportunities to hit the volley. The server can get to the net faster behind the serve by quickly taking a couple of steps after the serve and before the split step. By having his or her partner return the serve or feed a return, the server can get a better feel for the serve and quick close without fear of losing a point in a match or wasting another team's time.

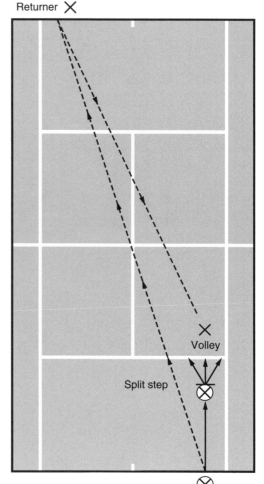

1. Players get into position, one on each side of the net.
2. The server serves hard to a specific target so the returner knows where the ball is going.
3. The returner prepares to return (or if feeding, has ball in hand).
4. The server comes forward as fast as possible to the net.
5. The returner returns the ball or feeds a ball just as the served ball passes him or her.
6. The server volleys the ball cross court as close to the net as possible.

Other areas that the server can practice include the timing of the split step, the placement of the serve, and varying the speed and spin of the serve. The server may also want to work on hitting the first volley more aggressively, hitting the first volley deeper, being decisive on the second or third volleys, and hitting half-volleys.

Split Step

This drill helps players learn to move quickly toward the net and be on balance to move to hit volleys. The server will generally, but not always, take three steps before the split step.

1. Players get into position, one on each side of the net.
2. The server performs a serve movement without hitting a ball.
3. The server takes two explosive steps and one slower step in the direction of the simulated serve.
4. The returner, holding a ball in his hand, moves the ball to one side or the other.
5. The server split steps and moves in the direction that the partner has moved the ball.
6. Repeat the drill with the server actually serving the ball and the returner feeding a ball.
7. Repeat the drill with the server actually serving the ball and the returner actually returning it.

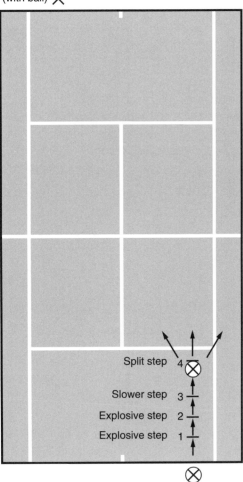

Close Serving, Quick Return

In this drill the server should serve from somewhere between the service line and the baseline, so that the ball gets to the player returning serve sooner and therefore requires a quicker reaction and more efficient preparation on the part of the returner. Practicing this way makes a normal serve look as if it is coming in slow motion. Coaches who are getting older and cannot serve as hard can use this drill to work a player hard and help him or her learn to prepare for the serve quickly.

1. Players get into position, one on each side of the net.
2. The returner selects a target area for the return.
3. The server stands several feet inside the baseline and serves normally.
4. The returner tries to hit the ball into the target area.

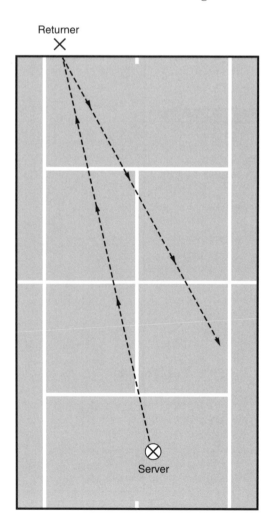

After practicing the serve and the return of serve with your partner, use the following drills to improve other aspects of your doubles game.

Closing

In this drill, players work on hitting the ball on the move as both players rush toward the net.

1. Players get into position, one on each side of the net.
2. Players stand at opposite baselines with several balls in their pockets.
3. A player starts the action by feeding a ball deep toward the other baseline and moving toward the net.
4. The other player moves forward, takes that ball in the air, and volleys it back.
5. Both players hit volleys or half-volleys while continuing to move forward until someone misses or gets hit (this happens occasionally). Players then backpedal to their original positions and repeat steps 3 through 5.

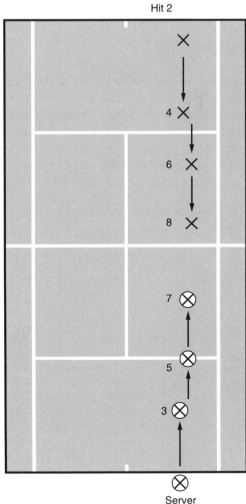

Hit 2

Server
(Hit or feed 1)

The closing drill simulates the doubles point in that neither player knows how or from where the ball is going to be hit. They have to make instantaneous adjustments to the ball and their opponent, and determine where and how to hit the next shot. Players must decide quickly whether to hit the ball before it bounces, as a volley, or just after it bounces, as a half-volley. The closer they get to the net and their opponent, the more careful the players must be to keep the ball low and, of course, the less time they have to react to the next shot. To return the ball low, from a low volley, a player must take some pace off the ball so that it goes over the net but then is low for the opponent. The potential penalty for hitting it too high is a tattoo somewhere on the body from your friendly practice partner (don't blame him or her; you set it up). You can do the closing drill by moving straight forward on half of the court or by hitting cross court as you would most likely be doing in doubles.

Deep Volleys

In this variation of the closing drill, the two players stand at the service line and volley. The goal is to hit most of the volleys to the practice partner at about chest level, which means that if balls are not hit, they will land around the baseline. This encourages firm, deep volleying, which is vital in doubles. Players can move forward a little bit but should not close as they did in the previous drill. This drill works on reactions and footwork, and also strengthens the forearm and wrist as it encourages firm, deep volleys.

1. Players get into position, one on each side of the net, at the service line.
2. Players hit firm volleys back and forth at chest level.
3. The object is to keep the ball going as long as possible.

One Up, One Back

This is a good drill for improving movement at net. It also gives players practice with overheads and practice reacting to change of pace shots.

1. One player takes a basket of balls to the baseline; the other sets up near, but on the opposite side of, the net.
2. The player at the baseline hits drives, dinks, and lobs to the person playing the net.
3. The net player tries to hit each ball deep, back to the player at the baseline, before it bounces.
4. The baseline player varies the shots so that the net player does not know what is coming. The baseline player should use difficult combinations, such as a deep lob followed by a little dink shot at the net player's feet.

   This one up, one back drill allows the net player to work on technique, balance, quick movement, and adjustment and recovery. It is also a conditioning opportunity; if the drill is done properly, the net player will usually not last more than about five minutes before needing a rest or rotation.

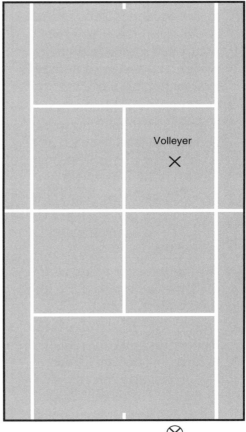

Baseline player

Catch, Hit, and Drop

One of the important ingredients in a good doubles player is the ability to adjust to the pace of the ball, especially when at the net. As I mentioned in chapter 6, it takes soft hands to receive those hard balls and to control the return shot. How does a player get soft hands? This drill conveys the idea of holding the racket lightly. It is a progressive drill, and players should work on the catch part first. A coach could take the role of the feeder.

1. Players stand in volleying position on either side of the net, just inside the service line.

2. One player, the feeder, tosses or hits a ball softly to the other player.

3. The receiving player tries to "catch" the ball on his racket. This means that the receiver lets the racket come back with the ball as the ball connects with the racket, so that the ball does not bounce off the strings but stays on them. This is a little like a lacrosse player receiving the ball in the net and then throwing it back. The receiver should hold the racket lightly and sort of "go with the pitch." It takes some time to get the hang of this move.

4. Once the receiver understands how to catch the ball, the feeder will call out just after each feed whether the player is to catch the ball or hit it as a volley.

5. The volleyer must prepare to volley every ball but be ready to adjust to the command of the feeder.

6. During the next phase of the drill, the feeder asks for a few drop volleys.

7. During the final phase, the feeder calls out for the receiver to catch, hit, or drop (drop volley) each shot, while the ball is in the air. For more of a challenge, the feeder can delay issuing the command.

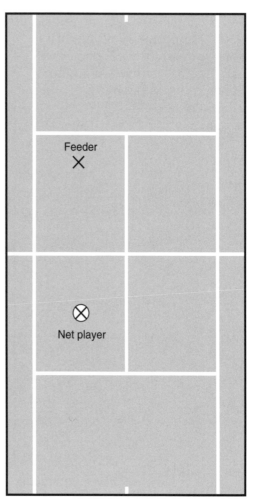

Alternate Deep and Short Volley

This drill helps players develop a feel for the difference between hitting a deep volley and hitting a short volley. A coach could take the role of the feeder.

1. Players get into position, one on each side of the net. One player, the feeder, should have a basket of balls.
2. The player with the basket of balls feeds shots to the volleyer.
3. The volleyer alternates hitting deep and short volleys, mixing in an occasional drop volley.
4. The volleyer should concentrate on adjusting the power of the volley according to the length of shot.

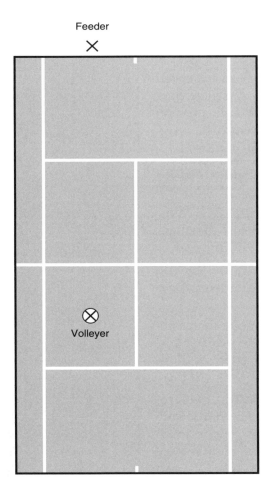

Drills With Another Team or Coach

There are several drills that can be done with another team or with a coach. Be sure to cooperate fully with the other doubles team, which could be another team on your USTA League Team or a school or club team. You can help them in some areas of their game, and they can help you with a few areas of your game.

Poaching

One area that you must work on with another team is poaching. This requires at least three players, and ideally, four. It is best to start with a predictable return so that you can work on the timing of the poaching. As the drill progresses, the returning team can vary the return as they would do in a match. Once you understand when to move, you will be much more effective at poaching. With practice, you will learn to judge the various factors involved such as the speed and spin of the serve, the placement of your partner's serve, the position of your opponent returning serve, and your own ability to move.

1. Teams get into position for doubles play.

2. The server serves cross court, and the returner hits all returns cross court.

3. The net player on the serving team poaches to intercept the return.

4. After several consecutive cross-court returns, the returner varies the location and type of return.

5. Throughout this drill, the serving team should communicate whether or not to poach on each point. The server should vary the speed and spin of each serve.

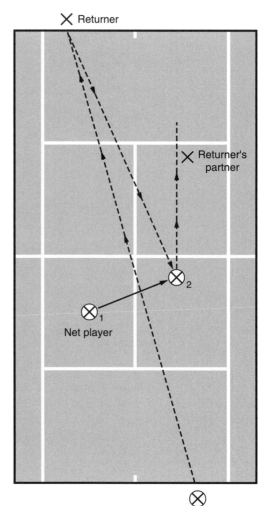

Acquiring the ability to poach while serving will make you a much better team; your opponents will be wondering what you're planning to do when they are returning serve. They will miss some returns because they are thinking about and looking at you instead of the ball.

Returning Team Poach

Once you understand poaching from the serving team's point of view, you can try poaching when your partner is returning serve. If your partner hits a low return of serve, you can try to intercept the low volley or half-volley. This may cause the opponents to look up when they are volleying instead of watching the ball closely. Even if they don't miss that first volley, knowing that you might cross at any time puts more pressure on them. The following drill helps players learn when and where to poach off of the return of serve.

1. Teams get into position for doubles play.
2. The server hits the second serve and comes to the net.
3. The returner hits the return cross court.
4. The serving team hits a volley cross court.
5. The returner's partner poaches, and the returner covers the open court.
6. The server hits a volley anywhere.

If the practice team can serve and volley second serves so that you can execute good returns, you can work on when and how to cross. When you cross, your partner should cover the area behind you in case the opponents put the volley there.

Run Around Backhand Return and Poach

Practice running around the backhand on the second serve and hitting forehands that dip down to your opponent's feet; this makes it easier for you to poach. If you run around the serve on the deuce side as I did playing with Bob Lutz, you should continue to move toward the middle. If your partner poaches, then naturally you will cover the other half of the court. Bob and I would talk to each other before the serve and make a plan; we might say that if I got a second serve I would try to get it low with my forehand and that he would cross. It took a while for us to understand exactly how to pull it off, but this strategy proved very effective for us, especially on some important points. The following drill helps teams learn to use a strong forehand and to poach on the return.

1. Teams get into position for doubles play.
2. The server hits a second serve into the middle of the service box and comes to the net.
3. The returner moves to the left as the serve is hit and returns the ball cross court.
4. The server hits a volley cross court.
5. The returner's partner poaches.
6. The returner moves across to cover for the poacher.

Lob Return

When you practice hitting defensive lobs against another team, you can experiment and discover the most ideal positioning to assume after you have hit a lob. If you hit a high lob deep and down the middle, then it's best to leave room in the middle of your formation to entice your opponents into hitting toward the middle. If they hit the ball in that area, then you will probably be able to get your racket on the ball and keep the point going.

1. Teams get into position for doubles play.
2. The server serves while the returner and the returner's partner stay back.
3. The returner lobs the return of serve high and down the middle.
4. The net player or the server hits an overhead.
5. The returner and the returner's partner position themselves so that they leave a gap in the center of their formation.

Use these practice matches to try different tactics and to communicate about what works and what does not work. If you can get a coach to work with you as you play your practice matches, then you will probably improve even more quickly and understand the concepts even better. The coach can also help orchestrate the matches so that the two teams work together efficiently and cooperatively.

Practicing with a purpose will help you improve, as an individual player and as a team. It can be fun to try some new tactics and to strive to reach your doubles potential.

Index

About the Author

Courtesy of the author

Stan Smith has played or coached tennis at the professional level for more than 30 years. He has won the most prestigious tournaments in both singles and doubles and has coached elite players and juniors. From 1988 to 1995 Smith served as director of coaching for the USTA Player Development Program, and in 2000 he was the head coach of the men's U.S. Olympic team at the Sydney Olympics.

Smith has played in 11 Grand Slam finals and has won a remarkable 61 pro doubles titles. He has a 12–1 Davis Cup doubles record, and he's a four-time U.S. Open doubles winner. He and his frequent doubles partner, Bob Lutz, are the only team ever to have won the national championship on all four surfaces.

Smith has been a contributing editor of *Tennis* magazine for 19 years, is the author of *Inside Tennis*, and is coauthor of *Modern Doubles.* He has been the touring tennis pro at Sea Pines Resort since 1971, and he still plays doubles in the senior Grand Slam events, where he continues to enjoy competing against some very familiar rivals. He and his wife, Margie, live in Hilton Head, South Carolina.